D1545446

DATE DUE

WITHDRAWN

ORIGINS
OF THE
SAUDI ARABIAN OIL EMPIRE

Origins
Of The
Saudi Arabian Oil Empire

Secret U. S. Documents, 1923 — 1944

Edited and Introduced
by
Nelson Robertson

Documentary Publications
Salisbury, North Carolina, U.S.A.
1979

INTRODUCTION

Today's oil crisis holds every promise of causing more damage to world economic, social and political order than any other force acting upon human history. It is more threatening to world peace than even the forty-five year old Cold War.

While the immediate cause of current world instability is universally regarded as stemming from the OPEC oil price increases beginning in 1973, the origins of the present crisis antedate these developments by some fifty years.

The true beginnings of the world oil crisis might best be traced to the year 1923, when an unknown New Zealand promoter and an all-but-unknown tribal chieftain entered into an agreement to search for oil in the deserts of the Arabian peninsula. Major Frank Holmes was perhaps the very first westerner to sense the oil riches under the desert wastes of Arabia, and certainly the very first to take positive efforts to exploit this wealth. Although badly underfinanced and unable to speak a word of Arabic, Major Holmes formed a small British syndicate, then went to Arabia to seek out the victorious leader of the Wahabi tribes who had proclaimed himself several years earlier the King of the Nejd. That king was Abdul Aziz ibn Saud, a brilliant desert warrior who in the years ahead was to unify all central Arabia under his leadership. But in 1923, ibn Saud had won barely a toehold in the Nejd regions, and he was desperate for funds to enable him to consolidate his position on the peninsula.

In these years only the Anglo-Persian Oil Company was of importance in Middle East oil production. Its principal efforts were being profitably carried on in Persia, and there was no interest in the oil potential of Arabia. Sir Arnold Wilson, then General Manager of the Anglo-Persian Oil Company, made no effort to protect his company's unique position in the Middle East and once wrote that he personally

i

could not believe any oil was ever to be found in Arabia itself. That opinion may well have influenced King ibn Saud, for he himself is reported to have confided to his close friends that there was no oil ever to be found in commercial quantities in his domain. Ibn Saud's agreement with Major Holmes' syndicate was designed at its onset to bring in much needed capital in the name of royalty advances, but the King never dreamed that these royalties would ever be recaptured from operating oil wells in his kingdom.

Before any serious drilling could be undertaken, the Eastern and General Syndicate of Major Holmes ran out of funds. By 1924 operations were all but discontinued. Then in 1928, after lengthy negotiations, ibn Saud officially ended the syndicate's concession. Major Frank Holmes turned his attention to Bahrein, where he was later to strike oil and become a rich man. Yet all his efforts to convince King ibn Saud to reconsider his termination of the oil concessions failed, and Major Frank Holmes never again returned to the Kingdom of Nejd.

In the ensuing years the influence of Great Britain diminished in Arabia in almost direct proportion to the rise in power of ibn Saud. Gradually the British soldier, advisor and businessman was replaced in importance in central Arabia by the American. By 1933, when ibn Saud's Kingdom of Saudi Arabia received official recognition by Washington, American oil and business interests held the key position in central Arabia.

In 1932, the Standard Oil Company of California took over the dormant exploration concession of Major Holmes. By 1935, after several years of geological surveys, the first drilling was begun. The pace was slow and early results were discouraging. During the next three years only six wells were drilled, mostly to a depth of 3,200 feet, but none showed enough promise to warrant further development. Several of the company's geologists argued that oil must be deeper down, and the next well, Well No. 7, was pushed to the then unheard of depth of 4,700 feet. Early in the morning hours of March 5, 1938, oil blew out of Well No. 7 in a tremendous gusher. Using the words of St. John Philby, ibn Saud's closest European friend and advisor, that day "the lid was off."

The 51 documents in this collection cover these years and continue through World War II. All were selected from previously secret U.S. diplomatic files in the National Archives in Washington, D.C. None have been published before. The documents begin with the first notices of the oil concessions given to Major Holmes in 1923, cover the emergence of American oil companies and their role in the Middle East, the formation of the American-Arabian oil consortium known as ARAMCO, and close with materials on the role of Saudi oil in World War II.

The materials included emphasize the political, economic, geographic and diplomatic aspects of the early years of oil in Saudi Arabia. They have been carefully selected to represent the most important materials in U.S. secret files, but they are in no way to be considered as supplying the reader the complete picture of these years. Any such collection would require, in addition to American materials, documentation from the governmental archives of Great Britain and Saudi Arabia, along with the confidential files held by the oil corporations themselves. Unfortunately, such an ideal balance of basic source materials is not likely to be achieved. Neither the records of Great Britain and Saudi Arabia, nor those of the oil corporations, is open to scholars. And there is no prospect that such records will be made available in the foreseeable future.

Other documentary sources may prove helpful. One should consult Ibrahim al-Rashid's *Documents on the History of Saudi Arabia* which has appeared to date in five volumes (Salisbury, N.C., 1976 - 1979). These volumes provide many heretofore unpublished secret documents on the origins and development of ibn Saud's kingdom, covering the period from 1916 through 1950. Another newly-published two-volume collection edited by William Kennedy, *Secret History of the Oil Companies in the Middle East* (Salisbury, N.C., 1979) contains documents of great importance on the emergence of the economic and political power of American oil corporations in the Middle East, and in particular in Saudi Arabia, during the years immediately following the end of World War II.

There are other official source materials of value to the serious student. Certainly one to be consulted is the Federal Trade Commission's *The International Petroleum Cartel*, issued by the Select Committee on Small Business, U.S. Senate, 82nd Congress, 2nd Session (Washington, D.C., 1952). These hearings are of great value for tracing the role of U.S. oil corporations in the development of foreign economic and political policy. What little has been released by the Saudis can be found in the *First Memorial in Arbitration Proceedings between the Government of Saudi Arabia and Aramco, Geneva, 1956*. This memorial consists of various legal briefs, official Saudi documents, memoranda and actual arbitration proceedings. Bound copies have been deposited in the Hoover Institution at Stanford, California, where they are available to qualified scholars. In this connection, one should also consult *Petroleum Arrangements with Saudi Arabia,* a collection of materials published by the Special Committee Investigating National Defense Programs, U.S. Senate, 80th Congress, 1st Session (Washington, D.C., 1948).

No less important are the first-hand narratives and personal memoirs published by various participants and observers in these early years. H. St. John Philby, the brilliant Moslem convert and close friend and advisor to King ibn Saud, wrote several excellent if biased books. His *Arabian Jubilee* (London, 1952) and *Saudi Arabia* (New York, 1955) provide first-rate background on the rise of ibn Saud, his mind and philosophy, and his early contacts with the oil companies. Philby's final book, *Arabian Oil Ventures*, (Washington, D.C., 1964) which was published posthumously, may be the best single first-hand account of the early years of oil in Saudi Arabia.

Books by American advisors, friends of ibn Saud, and various promoters, may be used to balance those of St. John Philby. Several by Ameen Rihani are of value, since this Lebanese friend and advisor to ibn Saud had obtained U.S. citizenship and sold his information to the U.S. Department of State. Rihani was most probably America's "first spy" in the Middle East. His *Makers of Modern Arabia* (Boston, 1928) and *Around the Coasts of Arabia* (Boston, 1930) are of particular value for intimate facts on ibn Saud and his Court. One might also read Karl S. Twitchell's *Saudi Arabia* (Princeton, 1947), also based on extensive personal contact with Saudi Arabia and its leaders, but more scholarly than the works of Rihani.

Ameen Rihani, along with a missionary, Charles Crane, and the American engineer, Karl Twitchell, did much to turn ibn Saud's eyes from Europe to America. Though none participated directly in the oil concessions or the profits stemming from oil development, it is doubtful that American oil companies would have been given their early start in the Middle East without the efforts of these three generally unknown Americans.

Finally, a few words on the presentation of the 51 documents in this collection. Where possible I have tried to supply the original document in facsimile, even though this method has presented problems in clarity and in mechanical reproduction. I believe that the importance of this material requires that it be provided in as authentic a form as possible. An index has been provided at the end of the book. Since there are no specific chapters, readers interested in certain topics are referred first to the document headings in the Table of Contents and then to the index.

No claim is made here that this collection supplies the full and final documentation on the origins of the oil empire in Saudi Arabia. It is rather one attempt to place into the hands of interested students of the subject all those key materials available in United States archives which have not been published, and which are not readily available without extensive travel, research and expense. If this collection serves to advance the knowledge of this critical topic only one step, then its publication will have been worth while.

Nelson Robertson
Washington, D. C.

CONTENTS

vi

No. 220.

AMERICAN CONSULATE,

Bagdad, Iraq, June 7, 1923.

SUBJECT: Oil Concession in Nejd.

THE HONORABLE

THE SECRETARY OF STATE,

WASHINGTON.

SIR:

I have the honor to refer to the Department's telegraphic instruction of May 18, 1923 with regard to a concession which was reported to have been granted to Major Frank Holmes by the Sultan of Nejd.

About two months ago Major Holmes left Bagdad for Hasa where he expected to meet the Sultan. Before leaving he told me that he had a letter from Sir Percy Cox to the Sultan, leaving the latter free to give the concession to whomever he saw fit. At the same time Mr. Amin Rihani, American, who had just returned from Nejd informed me that the High Commissioner was using all his influence on behalf of the Anglo-Persian Oil Company, but the Sultan Ibn Saoud was very much in favor of Major Holmes' proposition, with certain modifications, one of which was that the concurrence of the Sultan must be obtained before the concession could be transferred to any other company. Major Holmes showed me the clause in his proposed terms relating to this question and told me that it would be impossible to enter into an agreement which did not leave the concessionaires free to transfer without refer-

reference to the Sultan.

When Major Holmes left here he seemed confident that all points of difference would be adjusted and that he would obtain the concession.   I heard nothing more about it until it was announced in the Bagdad Times that a concession embracing 40,000 square miles in the Hasa district of Nejd had been given to Major Holmes in the name of the Eastern and General Syndicate, London.

I saw the High Commissioner and incidentally referred to the concession.   He stated that he did not know the status of the matter as it was being handled from Bushire, but that he did not think the Sultan had yet made up his mind.   I next saw Abdul Latif Pasha, Minister of Aukaf, who is the Sultan's representative in Mesopotamia and he told me that he did not think the concession had been granted and that he had advised the Sultan to wait.   He also told me that Major Holmes had never told him much about the company he represents and that he himself had made direct inquiry from London and had found that the company was a small one having only L100,000 capital.   Neither Abdul Latif Pasha nor the High Commissioner remembered the name of the President of the Syndicate.   Consul General Tredwell heard in Basrah that the President is one of the Directors of the Anglo-Persian Oil Company, but this I am unable to confirm.

Sir Arnold Wilson was reported to have gone to Hasa about two weeks ago and it is presumed that he still has hopes of getting the concession.

Abdul Latif Pasha told me that he had advised Ibn Saoud to have a survey of the oil field made on his own account and determine what he has and then put it up to the highest bidder.   He wondered why some American company had not already made a bid for it.

As soon as further information can be obtained, I shall make another report on this subject.

I have the honor to be, Sir,

Your obedient servant,

Thomas R Owens

Thomas R. Owens
American Consul.

4

AMERICAN CONSULATE,

Aden, Arabia, June 20, 1923.

SUBJECT: Reported Oil Concession in Hasa Province of Nejd,

Arabia.

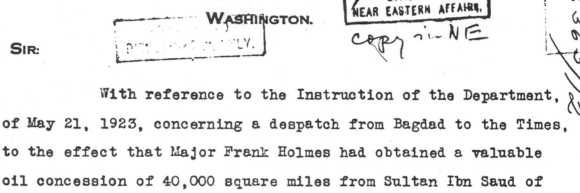

THE HONORABLE

THE SECRETARY OF STATE,

WASHINGTON.

SIR:

With reference to the Instruction of the Department,
of May 21, 1923, concerning a despatch from Bagdad to the Times,
to the effect that Major Frank Holmes had obtained a valuable
oil concession of 40,000 square miles from Sultan Ibn Saud of
the Nejd, I have the honor to report that it has proved impossible to obtain in Aden any information absolutely confirming
this.

Major Holmes is well known in Aden, however, and all
who read the article in the Times are of the opinion that it is
an accurate report. The manager of the English Pharmacy, Aden,
a subsidiary of the Eastern and General Syndicate, Limited,
claims to have received word from the home office at London that
the concession was about to be granted, and was not at all surprised by the report in the Times.

He confirms the statement that the Anglo Persia have
no interest in the concession. Although it is not known how much
oil there actually is in the concession, the Eastern and General
Syndicate is reported to have sufficient capital already available for immediate development.

DEPT. OF STATE

JUL 26 1923

ACKNOWLEDGED

I have the honor to be, Sir,

Your obedient servant,

Raymond Davis

Raymond Davis

American Consul.

File No. 863.

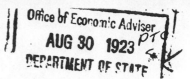

AMERICAN CONSULATE,

CONFIDENTIAL

Bagdad, Iraq, July 5, 1923.

SUBJECT: Oil Concession in Nejd.

THE HONORABLE

THE SECRETARY OF STATE,

WASHINGTON.

SIR:

I have the honor to acknowledge the receipt of the
Department's confidential instruction of May 21, 1923, relative
to the reported oil concession given by Ibn Saud, Sultan of
Nejd, to Major Frank Holmes for the Eastern and General Syn-
dicate, Limited, London, covering a large tract of land in the
Hasa district of Nejd.

In my despatch No.220 of June 7, 1923, relative to the
same subject, reference was made to incidental conversations
with the High Commissioner and with Abdul Latif Pasha, Ibn Saud's
representative in Mesopotamia. They indicated to me that no
agreement had been concluded, but it now appears that the concession was given as reported and that opposition on the part
of the Anglo-Persian Oil Company was mere camouflage. I am informed that Admiral Slade, who was in Mesopotamia about a year
ago, is the President of the Eastern and General Syndicate and
that he is the Government's representative on the board of the
Anglo-Persian Oil Company. This and several other things tend
to confirm a suspicion which I had that Major Holmes was working
indirectly for the British Government and the Anglo-Persian Oil
Company instead of against them as he took particular pains to

impress upon me. He told me several conflicting stories as to what was happening and on one occasion he told an American who happened to be in Bagdad en route to Teheran that he was out here in the interest of the Government.

Copy hereof is being forwarded to the American Embassy at London.

I have the honor to be, Sir,

Your obedient servant,

Thomas R Owens

Thomas R. Owens,
American Consul.

**EMBASSY OF THE
UNITED STATES OF AMERICA**

LONDON, July 24, 1923.

No. 2647

The Honorable

The Secretary of State,

Washington.

Sir:

With reference to your Instruction No. 925
of July 6, 1923, concerning the concession which
Major Frank Holmes is said to have procured for the
Eastern and General Syndicate, Limited, of London,
in the province of Hassa, Arabia, there is enclosed
herewith a copy of the last balance sheet of the
Company, setting forth their financial condition
as of August 31, 1921. This report was issued on

-2-

June 9, 1922, and on the front page it will be noted
that the issued capital since the date of the balance
sheet has been raised to £15,401.15.0d. The National
City Bank understands that the capital of the Eastern
was further increased by £75,000 on the 10th instant.

The Bank states that the Syndicate is believed
to be in good hands and trustworthy for its engagements, and that its bankers report that the account
with them has been satisfactorily conducted and has
shown substantial balances.

The principal shareholders appear to be Allen
and Hanburys, The Chartered and General Exploration and
Finance Company, Limited, W.H. Shelford and B. M.
Messa of Arabia. Of the Directors -

    Mr. Edmund Davis is a member of the firm
            of Jacob Picard & Company, foreign agents,
            27-8 Old Jewry. He is also associated
            as a Director with a very large number
            of mining and railway propositions.

    Mr. Edmund William Janson is of Percy Tarbutt
            and Company, consulting engineers, 18,
            St. Swithin's Lane, and is also a Director
            of numerous mining companies.

    Mr. F. W. Gamble is a Director of Allen and
            Hanburys, Limited, the well known chemists
            and manufacturers of patent foods, etc.

    Mr. J. E. H. Lomas is a member of the Institute
            of mining engineers, and has his office at
            32, Great St. Helens. He is likewise a
            Director of numerous mining, land and
            rubber companies.

    Mr. Percy C. Tarbutt is of Percy Tarbutt and
            Company, consulting engineers, and he also is
            connected with numerous trusts and syndicates
            of a mining character.

The Bank states that there appears to be no

connection between the Syndicates and the Anglo-Persian Oil Company.

I have the honor to be, Sir,

Your obedient servant,

Post Wheeler
Charge d'Affaires <u>ad interim</u>

Enclosure:
Balance Sheet of the
Eastern & General Syndicate,
Limited.

EASTERN & GENERAL SYNDICATE
LIMITED.

DIRECTORS' REPORT AND ACCOUNTS,
31st AUGUST, 1921.

NOTICE IS HEREBY GIVEN that the ORDINARY GENERAL MEETING of the Members of the above Company will be held at the Registered Office of the Company, No. 19, St. Swithin's Lane, London, E.C. 4, on Monday, the 19th day of June, 1922, at 2 o'clock p.m., to transact the ordinary business of the Company.

By order of the Board.

H. T. ADAMS,
Secretary.

19, St. Swithin's Lane,
London, E.C. 4,
9th June, 1922.

EASTERN & GENERAL SYNDICATE LIMITED.

CAPITAL.

Authorised :—£50,300 in 200,000 Ordinary Shares of 5s. each,
and 6,000 Deferred Shares of 1s. each.

Issued to date of this Report :—60,407 Ordinary Shares = £15,101 15 0

6,000 Deferred Shares =   300 0 0

£15,401 15 0

Directors.
EDMUND DAVIS.
F. W. GAMBLE.
E. W. JANSON.
J. E. H. LOMAS.
P. C. TARBUTT.

Bankers.
THE NATIONAL PROVINCIAL AND UNION BANK OF ENGLAND LIMITED,
2, Princes Street, London, E.C.

Solicitors.
HOLMES, SON & POTT.

Auditors.
J. DIX LEWIS, CÆSAR & CO.

Secretary.
H. T. ADAMS.

Office.
19, St. Swithin's Lane, London, E.C. 4.

REPORT OF THE DIRECTORS.

To be submitted to the Ordinary General Meeting to be held at the Office of the Company, No. 19, St. Swithin's Lane, London, E.C.4, on Monday, the 19th day of June, 1922, at 2 o'clock p.m.

The Directors submit herewith the audited Statement of Accounts for the period from the date of the incorporation of the Company, the 6th August, 1920, to the 31st August, 1921.

The Company was formed to deal with concessions in Arabia, with which object Major Frank Holmes and Lt.-Commander C. E. V. Craufurd proceeded to Arabia to look into several propositions that had been suggested.

The Company has opened in Aden, under efficient European management, a chemist's and druggist's business, from which, after the initial period, a satisfactory revenue is anticipated.

The Auditors, Messrs. J. DIX LEWIS, CÆSAR & Co., retire and do not offer themselves for re-election. It is proposed that Messrs. HUBBART, DUROSE & PAIN, of Atlantic House, 46, Holborn Viaduct, London, E.C. 1, should be elected Auditors for the ensuing year.

By order of the Board.

H. T. ADAMS,
Secretary.

19, ST. SWITHIN'S LANE,
    LONDON, E.C. 4,
        9th June, 1922.

EASTERN AND GENERAL SYNDICATE LIMITED.

(Incorporated the 6th day of August, 1920.)

Dr.   BALANCE SHEET, 31st AUGUST, 1921.   **Cr.**

	£ s. d.	£ s. d.		£ s. d.	£ s, d.
To Capital—			By Furniture and Fittings at cost		612 8 2
Authorised—			By Stock at Pharmacy at valuation		2,382 0 4
200,000 Ordinary Shares of 5s. each	50,000 0 0				
6,000 Deferred ,, 1s. ,,	300 0 0		By Cash—		
		£50,300 0 0	At Bankers, in hand and in transit—		
			London	525 13 11	
Issued—			Aden	641 17 5	
26,407 Ordinary Shares of 5s. each	6,601 15 0		In transit	39 19 0	
6,000 Deferred ,, 1s. ,,	300 0 0				1,207 10 4
		6,901 15 0	By Prospecting Expenditure in Arabia		2,159 18 1
To Creditors		1,063 0 4	By Sundry Expenditure—		
			LONDON—		
			Preliminary Expenses... ...	675 19 4	
			General Charges, Legal Charges, Office Expenses, Postages and Telegrams, Stationery and Printing	382 18 8	
				1,058 18 0	
			Deduct Interest received ...	61 2 9	
				997 15 3	
			ADEN—		
			Purchases of Stock for Pharmacy, Salaries and General Expenses, *less* Sales and Stock	605 3 2	
					1,602 18 5
		£7,964 15 4			**£7,964 15 4**

On behalf of the Board,

    EDMUND DAVIS, } *Directors.*
    E. W. JANSON, }

Report of the Auditors to the Shareholders of EASTERN AND GENERAL SYNDICATE LIMITED.

We have examined the Balance Sheet of the EASTERN AND GENERAL SYNDICATE LIMITED, dated 31st August, 1921, as above set forth. We have obtained all the information and explanations we have required. In our opinion such Balance Sheet is properly drawn up so as to exhibit a true and correct view of the state of the Syndicate's affairs according to the best of our information and the explanations given us.

We have accepted the statements of the Syndicate's representatives with regard to all expenditure abroad.

KENNAN'S HOUSE,
    CROWN COURT,
        CHEAPSIDE, E.C. 2,
  30th January, 1922.

J. DIX LEWIS, CÆSAR & CO.,
    Chartered Accountants, } *Auditors.*

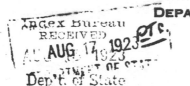

DEPARTMENT OF STATE
WASHINGTON

August 8, 1923.

Subject: Oil concession in Mesopotamia.

The Honorable

The Secretary of State,

Washington, D. C.

Sir:

I have the honor to refer to the Department's confidential instruction of May 21, 1923 (File No. 890 B. 6363-9) quoting a telegram received from the Embassy at London dated May 16, 1923, relating to an <u>oil concession</u> in the province of <u>Nejd Arabia</u> reported to have been received by <u>Major Frank Holmes</u> from Sultan Ibn Saud for the Eastern and General Syndicate, Limited, of London.

Mr. Amin Rihani, a naturalized American citizen of Syrian origin and a somewhat well known arabic writer recently came to Beirut after a journey through Arabia and Mesopotamia. He was the subject of a recent instruction from the Department requesting information regarding his movements.

Upon receipt of the Department's instruction under acknowledgment I sent for Mr. Rihani. He had been absent from the city but called at the Consulate a few days before my departure on leave of absence.

Mr. Rihani informed me during the course of our conversation that he had actually examined the document granting to Major Holmes the concession in question and had discussed the matter with Sultan Ibn Saud at the latter's request. While he did not recall the exact terms of the concession, he stated that it gave important and valuable privileges to the Eastern and General Syndicate, Limited, in the matter of the development of oil properties in Nejd. He stated further that he knew for a fact that the Anglo-Persian interests were bitterly opposed to the concession and tried to bring pressure to bear to prevent its award. He left Mesopotamia before the final consummation of the deal, and while he has had no further news of the matter he believes that it has certainly been put through by now.

I have the honor to be, Sir,

Your obedient servant,

American Consul, Beirut, Syria,
On leave of absence, temporarily
at Washington.

No 247

Office of Economic ...
PTC JAN 10 1924
DEPARTMENT OF STATE

AMERICAN CONSULATE,

Bagdad, Iraq, November 23, 1923.

SUBJECT: Advertisement of the Eastern Syndicate

DEPARTMENT OF STATE
DEC 22 1923
DIVISION OF
WESTERN EUROPEAN AFFAIRS

THE HONORABLE

THE SECRETARY OF STATE,

WASHINGTON.

SIR:

NOT TO BE PUBLISHED AS
OFFICIAL INFORMATION.

I have the honor to refer to my despatches Nos.220 and
225 of June 7, 1923, and July 5, 1923, respectively, and to
transmit for the information of the Department the following translation of an advertisement which appeared in the
Arabic section of the Times of Mesopotamia of November 6,1923;

"Notice is hereby given to all Nejdies residing
in Iraq, India and the Persian Gulf, that His
Highness the Sultan of Nejd and districts, has
concluded an agreement for oil concession in the
Hasa and Kateef zones, with the representatives
of the Eastern Syndicate Company.   It has been
decided that this company will consist of 300,000
shares, and the price per share will be one pound
sterling.   One fifth or 60,000 shares will be
the personal shares of His Highness while another
fifth or 60,000 shares will be offered for sale
to the subjects of His Highness who are residing
in Nejd and districts, Iraq, Syria, Hedjaz and
all other parts.   Since the conditions of the
said concession are of the most favorable terms
hitherto accepted by any other government, His
Highness, therefore, wishes that Nejdies should
not be kept out of this vital and useful affair,
hence, it is notified that all those desiring to
participate in the buying of shares alotted to
the subjects of His Highness, to proceed in re-
gistering their names at the Eastern Bank and
pay the value.   We do not think that the Nejdies
who are noted in their zeal for the promotion of
the interests of their homeland, involving personal gains as well, will loose this invaluable
opportunity as the remaining shares are about to

-2-

be exhausted.
Agent of His Highness the Sultan of Nejd."

The "Times of Mesopotamia" in commenting on the above advertisement said editorally, "Today is published elsewhere in Arabic in this issue an advertisement of the Eastern Syndicate, an oil company in Hasa and adjacent territories. No indication is given however as to where the head-office of the new company is. Intending investors have not the satisfaction of knowing the names of the Board of Directors, nor are the prospects of finding oil clearly indicated."

[Some think that the words of the Times are inspired by Sir Arnold Wilson of the Anglo-Persian Oil Company, but it is still believed by others that the concession practically belongs to the Anglo-Persian Oil Company. The whole question of that concession is not very clear.]

I have the honor to be, Sir,

Your obedient servant,

Thomas R. Owens
American Consul.

No. 11.

AMERICAN VICE CONSULATE.

Bushire, Persia.   May 25, 1924.

CONFIDENTIAL.

SUBJECT: Oil Concession in Nejd.

THE HONORABLE
    THE SECRETARY OF STATE
        WASHINGTON.

    Sir;

    I have the honor to acknowledge the receipt of
the Department's instruction of December 18, 1923 -
enclosing copies of a despatch from Bagdad relative to
an oil concession in Nejd, and to give the following
information on that subject, although much of it is
merely corroboratory. Most of this information has
been received from a British subject, the agent of the
Standard Oil Company. The source in particular,
should be kept confidential.

CONCESSIONAIRE

    The concessionaire is the Eastern & General
Syndicate, Ltd., London, represented by Major Frank
Holmes. The amount of its capital and the names of
the directors are not known, but could be ascertained
from the articles of association filed in Somerset House,
London.

-2-

THE CONCESSION

The length of the concession and the terms are not known, except that Ibn Saud can transport his troops in an emergency., on a railroad which is being contemplated. The concession was originally for 48,000 square miles, but it was increased in March by an additional 1,500 square miles, (the Times of Mesopotamia reports this to be 2,000 additional square miles). This new concession has been granted by the joint agreement of the Sultan of Nejd and the Sheikh of Koweit, and it is located in the Neutral Zone created by Sir Percy Cox at the Ojair Boundry Conference in December,1922. This Neutral Zone lies between the province of Hassa and the territory of the Sheikh of Koweit.

No further indications of oil are known to exist along the Arabian coast.

OPERATIONS

Major Holmes stated in March that evidence of oil had been discovered about 50 miles inland from Bahrein, in the mountainous district of Nejd. He went to Bagdad at that time to meet an American geologist and an American driller who were coming to make further examinations. He stated that no tests had yet been made. At that time there were no indications of oil in Koweit.

It is now reported in the press, that a Swiss geologist, Dr. Heim, with three assistants, began drilling the middle of April, sinking test holes in both the Neutral Zone and in the northern part of the previous concession in Hassa.

RELATIONS WITH BRITISH GOVERNMENT

The recent extension of the concession is reported to be with the consent of the Colonial Office.

It is generally agreed that there is no real competition between the Eastern & General Syndicate, and the Anglo-Persian Oil Company. A.T. Wilson tried to get the same concession for the latter company, and also tried to get a concession in Koweit. His failure seems not to worry anyone, and may have been more or less deliberate. It is generally reported that Admiral Slate, who was the government's representative on the Anglo-Persian Board, is at least a Director of the Eastern and General Syndicate, but this report cannot be verified here.

TRANSPORTATION TO THE FIELDS

El Khatiff is the present port of Hassa, where some of the drilling is now going on. However these fields are near El Hofuf, so the port that will eventually be used will be Ukair. It is planned to construct a railroad from the coast to these fields.

Further information will be reported.

A copy of this is being sent to the American Embassy in London, and one to the American Consul, Baghdad.

I have the honor to be, Sir,

Your obedient servant.

George Gregg Fuller

GEORGE GREGG FULLER
American Vice Consul

No 12.

891.6363

AMERICAN VICE CONSULATE.

Bushire, Persia. May 31, 1924.

SUBJECT;   The Nejd Oil Concession.

CONFIDENTIAL:

THE HONORABLE

   THE SECRETARY OF STATE

      WASHINGTON.

Sir;

    I have the honor to refer to my Despatch No 11,
dated May 25, 1924, which reported on the British Oil
Concession in Nejd.

    Although, as reported in the despatch referred to,
the general opinion is that the Eastern and General
Syndicate, and the Anglo-Persian Oil Company are working
together in securing the concession in Nejd from Ibn Saud
and the Sheikh of Koweit, still the British residents of
Basra and Bushire with whom I have talked, sincerely
believe that there is actual competition between these
two British companies. They say that the Anglo-Persian
Company were really disappointed at not receiving the
concession. This point could be more definitely settled
if it were known definitely that Admiral Slade is
connected with the newer company.

    The British Resident of the Persian Gulf believes
that Sasoons, of London, are financing the Eastern and
General Syndicate.

-2-

The failure of the Anglo Persian to secure this concession is reported by the British Resident to be due to the fear lest the British government grow too powerful in the oil field. He says that such fear is stupid, for the British government would take over any private British holdings if it ever required them. I suggested that perhaps the real reason was that they thought the fields would be more quickly developed by a private company which would have to show some returns to its investors, whereas a government might merely hold the fields for future use.

Until a few days ago there was no information obtainable in Bushire, Basra or Mohammerah that any oil had been discovered in the test drilling near Hassa or Koweit. However the British are very reticent about discussing oil.

A copy of this Despatch is being sent to the American ~~Legation~~ Embassy London.

I have the honor to be, Sir,

Your obedient servant.

GEORGE GREGG FULLER
American Vice Consul.

File No.

GGF/AAR

DEPT. OF STATE

SEP 29 1924

Division of
Foreign Service Administration

Department of State

OCT 1 1924

Division of
Political and Economic Information

DEPARTMENT OF STATE

SEP 26 1924

DIVISION OF
NEAR EASTERN AFFAIRS

COPY IN NEA

Office of Economic Adviser

SEP 27 1924

DEPARTMENT OF STATE

FURTHER RUMORS REGARDING THE NEJD OIL CONCESSION

George Gregg Fuller

From American Vice Consul

Bushire, Persia.

Date of Preparation: August 19, 1924.

Date of Mailing: August 23, 1924.

890B.6363/20

FILED OCT 3 1924 A

NEA INDEX BUREAU

According to remarks dropped by various British officials here, the concessionaires of the Nejd oil resources, are energetically pushing their scheme. Plans are now being formulated for the construction of a railway from the coast into the interior. Much interest is shown locally in the possible commercial development of Nejd and the Arabian coast if oil is found in paying quantities.

The opinion is generally expressed that the Eastern and General Syndicate, even if it is now seemingly in competition with the Anglo-Persian Oil Company, will combine with the latter when the preliminary work has been completed.

Source of Information:

British officials.

File No; 863.

GGF/AAR.

AMERICAN CONSULATE,

BAGDAD   IRAQ

MAY 3 1926

April 15, 1926.

SUBJECT: MAJOR HOLMES' OIL CONCESSION IN NEJD SAID TO HAVE ELAPSED.

Office of Economic Adviser
MAY 6 1926
DEPARTMENT OF STATE

For Distribution

THE HONORABLE

THE SECRETARY OF STATE,   Embassy   London

WASHINGTON.

890.F.6363/21

INDEX BUREAU

SIR:

I have the honor to refer to Consul Thomas R. Owen's despatches Nos. 220 and 225 of June 7 and July 5, 1923, entitled: "OIL CONCESSION IN NEJD," concerning the concession granted by Ibn Saud, Sultan of Nejd, to Major Frank Holmes for the Eastern & General Syndicate, Limited, London, covering a large tract of land in the Hasa district of Nejd, and to report as follows:

Indirectly but from what seems to be a very reliable authority, I learn that Major Frank Holmes considers that his oil concession in Nejd, granted to him in 1923 by Ibn Saud, has lapsed.   It is said that, in order to get this concession in the first place, Major Holmes was obliged to pay Ibn Saud a considerable sum of money in cash and also to give him an expensive motor car. It appears that no attempt has been made to do any actual drilling and that now Ibn Saud is demanding more money and further presents from Major Holmes if the concession is to remain in force.   I am informed that apparently the money and presents are not forthcoming and it was when speaking about the new demands of Ibn Saud that Major Holmes remarked that his concession had lapsed.

This information comes to me from a perfectly reliable friend who cannot be quoted but who stated to me that Major Holmes had made the above remarks in his presence.

Major Holmes is actually attempting to find oil in the Bahrein Islands, Persian Gulf, and it is reported that under this concession some drilling has been done and excellent artesian wells found but no oil as yet.

I have the honor to be, Sir,

Your obedient servant,

John Randolph,
American Consul.

File No. 863.6
JR/MD

NO. 204

AMERICAN CONSULATE,

Aden, Arabia.

January 28, 1927.

SUBJECT: Petroleum Operations in the Red Sea.

THE HONORABLE

THE SECRETARY OF STATE,

WASHINGTON.

/22

I have the honor to report, with reference
to despatch No. 172 of August 19, 1926, entitled "Prospective
Petroleum Operations in the Red Sea", that The Eastern and
General Syndicate, Limited, represented in Asir and Aden by Lt.-
Commander C. Crawford (Royal Indian Marine, retired), to
whom an oil concession in the Farsan Islands had been granted
by the Idrissi, lost this concession through their failure
to make the second payment when due, and that the Idrissi,
seizing this opportunity to tear up the contract in favor
of a more attractive offer made in the meantime by the
Anglo-Saxon Oil Company, promptly invited the Syndicate to
retire and immediately made the contract with the new firm.

Two articles on this subject, both appaearing in
the January 13, 1927 issue of the weekly English periodical
"The Near East and India", are enclosed, the first relating
the reported facts and describing the "romance" of the trans-
action, and the other giving the editorial view of the matter.
The story as reported by the Jeddah correspondent of the
weekly is not necessarily exact in all of the details, part-

icularly with regard to moneys paid and promised. The essential facts are, however, that the Eastern and General Syndicate, Limited, was unable to make good its agreement at the time stipulated, that it was in fact superseded by the Anglo-Saxon Oil Company, that oil occurs, probably in commercial quantities, in the Farsan Islands and that the prospective oil operations may be regarded as sufficiently lucrative to have justified the payment of a substantial total sum for the concession.

It has long been a recognized truth that petroleum exists in Farsan Islands, and the failure of European interests to take active measures for its development may be attributed to British surveillance and control of the Red Sea, rendered especially effective with respect to Farsan Islands through British ownership of the neighboring island of Kamaran, and to the troubled political status of Arabia during and since the war, 1914-1919, in the presence of which it would have been unsound from a business point of view to invest heavily in islands whose ownership was disputed.

Great Britain early took steps to secure the advantageous position at Kamaran which they now possess. The British had practical control of the Red Sea since their occupation of Aden in 1840, and did not definitley claim or use the island of Kamaran until Germany's policy of "Weltpolitik" and Germany's flowering navy were employed, as long ago as 1902, to make this island their own. This Consulate has lately been informed of the incident by an elderly Italian physician named Dr. A. Lanzoni, for many years the Resident at Assab, Eritrea and for thirty years a close student of Red Sea politics, but now in disfavor with the Fascist Government,

who passed this way en route to Abyssinia, in December, 1926.
Dr. Lanzoni stated that he himself saw, at Kamaran in 1902,
a German officer named Grapou, accompanied by one officer
and 11 soldiers of the Imperial German Marines, landing at
Kamaran from a small coaling ship named "Marie" to examine the
island. Grapou then landed a quantity of coal on Kamaran,
labeled it "Kaiserlich" coal and reloaded a portion of the same
coal before departing. The coincidence was that Grapou was
the Commander of a German naval ship which was also named "Marie".
The British Government (presumably the Aden authorities), learning
of this immediately dispatched a British war vessel called
"Perseus" to the island, to take official possession of it
and to prepare to establish a Residential government and a
coaling station. The exact details of subsequent events are
not clear, but the fact remains that Kamaran today is an un-
disputed British possession, the control of which is vested
in an officer and a detachment of troops from the Royal Indian
Army battalion stationed at Aden. The British action was
sufficiently decisive, apparently, to forestall not only the
Germans, but the Italians as well, since the latter sent, too
late, their ship "Berberigo" to investigate conditions.

Oil was the immediate object of the Germans, according
to Dr. Lanzoni, but there was the greater inducement of fixing
a valuable base of operations in the Red Sea and having an
island in a commanding position, to facilitate surveillance of
Arabian politics, and to assist in maintaining a dominant
position in the general Red Sea area, a position now undeniably
held by Great Britain.

The sketch map on the following page is intended to
illustrate the inter-relationships of Farsan Islands, Kamaran

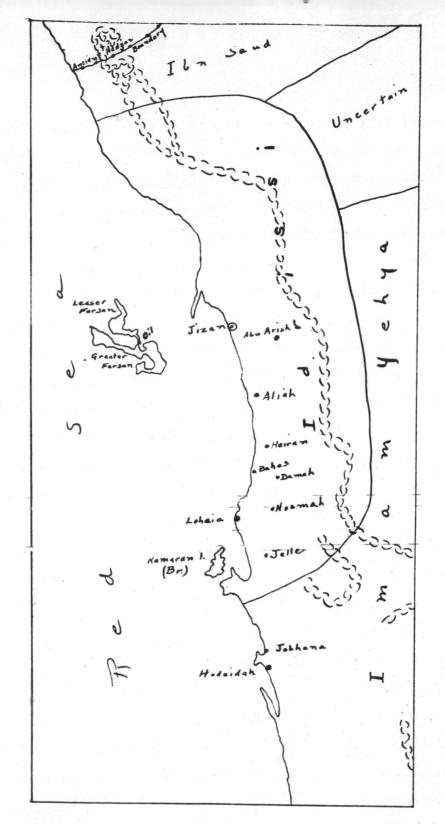

Relationships of the oil-bearing Farsan Islands
in the Red Sea, the oil of which was conceded
to the Anglo-Saxon Oil Company (British), the
British Island of Kamaran, the territories of
the British-supported Idrissi, the probable
frontier of Ibn Saud, friendly to Great Britain,
and that of the Imam of Yemen, who regards the
Idrissi as a foreigner and intruder, occupying
a portion of the /last several words illegible/

-5-

Island, the probable extent of Idrissi influence and the latter's territorial contacts with the Imam of Yemen abd Ibn Saud.

The same informant*cast some interesting light upon the manner in which petroleum appeared in Farsan Islands. It seems that the northern island (Farsan "Saghir" or Lesser Farsan) nearly meets the southern (Farsan "Kabir" or Greater Farsan) at a certain eastward point, and is separated from it by shallow water only at high tide. When the tide is at ebb, crude oil is seen to appear, seeping through the madreporic bed of the little strait thus denuded, and quickly filling the hollows

Seepage in Bed of Shallow Strait, Exposed at Low Water.

occurring there. From time immemorial the natives of the islands have been in the habit of collecting this oil for use as cooking fuel and in their primitive dip lamps. Fishermen gathered the oil in five-gallon tins, and sold it in the bazars at the nominal price of from 1 to 2 guerohe** per tin. The islands, it is observed, are coral formations, like the other islands and the greater part of the bed of the Red Sea***. It is yet to be seen by actual boring, which is reported to have been commenced, whether or not oil exists underneath the Red Sea in substantial

---

* [Dr. Lanzoni has in the past been helpful to this Consulate. He accompanied and materially assisted Mr. Southard in the preparation of the special report on Eritrea (No. 82 of 1920).]
** Guerohe: 1/20th of a Maria Theresa thaler, or 2½¢.
*** The Red Sea took its name in ancient times from the faint reddish hue of its coral bed.

quantities, but it would seem that production, if feasible, will soon be effected. There have been reports of oil indications in various parts of Arabia and East Africa, more especially in Mokalla (despatch 5), Abyssinia and British Somaliland (despatch 92) and the Egyptian coast of the Red Sea (the present enclosure).

A brief reference is made to the closing chapter of the history of the Eastern & General Syndicate, Limited. The Jeddah correspondent of the weekly periodical quoted, regards the Imam of Yemen as being "depressed and melancholy", because of the double threat to his independence and power, from the Italians on the one hand and the Idrissi on the other, and he makes a "romantic" story of the power of oil, especially since Farsan oil seems to have strengthened the Idrissi's hand and emboldened him to prepare for a war against the Imam. If the encouragement of strife in Arabia, and the encouragement of the loosely associated coastal tribes against the ruler of Yemen, to which natural division of Arabia those tribes historically, geographically and ethnologically belong, is "romantic", the Jeddah correspondent's intrepretation may be accepted. Certain it is, that the Eastern & General Syndicate, Limited, and, from a personal point of view, Commander Crawford, found no romance in it. His ruin is of no particular significance in this study, but it is of interest, as the personal touch ever is.

Commander Crawford took an active part in the formation and fxxx activities of the Eastern & General Syndicate, Limited, which established an office in Aden in the form of a drug store in 1920, to serve as camouflage and to cover its own expenses. For some reason, secrecy was closely observed throughout. Commander Crawford retired from the Royal Indian Marine soon after the Armistice, electing to take his pension in a lump sum, all

of which he invested in the new company, together with a
Major Holmes and other Englishmen who had capital to invest.
For six years there was much coming and going between England,
Aden and Jizan (Gheizan), without any definite result, owing
to unremittant political unrest, to changes in the rulers of
Asir, encroachments of the Imam, and to inability to meet the
Idrissi's terms. The capital of the Syndicate was not large
enough to compete with the Idrissi's ambitious demands. Like
all Arabs, when he found that he had something for which there
was a market, his price at once soared to dizzy and unreasonable
heights. Differences of opinion were finally encompassed by
Commander Crawford, who obtained a concession from the Idrissi
in the spring of 1926, paying the first instalment as agreed.
Crawford made a trip to Jizan last July, which seemed to
be most encouraging in its results. He went to London to
arrange for further payments and actual operations in Farsan,
returning in October, 1926, when he proceeded for the last time
to Jizan, to report that the second payment would be delayed,
and asked an extension of time for cash payment, by virtue of
the fact that British munitions were even then being landed at
Jizan for the Idrissi. This, he hoped, would be taken as a
mark of good faith, and was in fact a portion of the second
instalment. To his chagrin and bitter disappointment, Crawford
then learned that the Idrissi had already repudiated the concession
to the Syndicate, and was in the act of negotiating with the
Anglo-Saxon Oil Company, without having any intention of re-
funding moneys paid or compensating the Syndicate. All of the
Syndicate's ready cash had been used, and apparently certain
promised capital had been withdrawn. In its weakened state,
the Syndicate was easily supplanted by the Anglo-Saxon Oil

Company, which was able to pay more money and supply more
munitions, which, apparently, were on the spot, ready for
landing. The Idrissi (at present Seyed Hassan, uncle of the
deposed heir apparent, Seyed Ali), working with Seyed Mustapha
and the same Jamal Pasha who had come to Aden with Crawford,
could not resist seizing the excuse at hand to tear up his
contract with the Syndicate, and he calmly turned his back
to Crawford when the latter sought to save the concession last
October and November.

Commander Crawford returned to Aden in November, 1926,
still hoping against hope that his Syndicate would take some
step to save the day, possibly through proposing to merge with
the stronger Anglo-Saxon Oil Company, but he learned soon
enough of the withdrawal of the Syndicate, the prompt liquidation
of the Aden drug store by sale to London manufacturing chemists
named Allen & Hanbury, and the loss of his own small fortune.
He returned to England about the middle of December, a ruined
man, wondering what he could possibly do to earn a living. It
had been his hope to establish a source of revenue through the
oil business, which would leave him free to carry on the work
in which he is most interested, namely, the exploration and
archaeological study of Arabia, regarding which country already
he knows as much as any man living. His present plan is to
                    or archaeologists
endeavor to interest capitalists/of any nationality in making
expeditions into Yemen to seek and interpret the remnants of
the old Sabaean dynasty and into Hadramaut, to explore the ancient
city of Ophir, the greater Land of Ophir and the still untrodden
Empty Quarter.   He is a man of unusual brain power, and it is
sad that his scientific ability has thus been restrained, but

his failure is due to his simple faith in the word of an irresponsible Arab. He was the wrong man to deal with the Idrissi, because, like so many men of a high grade of mentality, vision and imagination, he was ill-suited to drive a bargain or conduct the business end of the oil project. He was even deceived by Jamal Pasha, with and through whom most of his negotiations with the Idrissi were carried on. Jamal Pasha, it seems, has been an artillery commander in Ibn Saud's army and is credited with being the present commander-in-chief of the Idrissi's forces.

The oil incident has served to expose just a little more of the careful collusion between the British, Ibn Saud and the Idrissi, against the Imam as the natural foe of all. And the pity of it all is that the Imam himself has no desire to oppose either Ibn Saud or the Aden Government. As between the Turks and the British, the Imam observed strict neutrality during the war, 1914-1919, but in spite of this, the Idrissi managed to obtain British recognition of his independence and of his title to the Farsan Islands, by means of a treaty in 1917, which at once arrayed the British against the Imam, who desires to absorb all of the territory occupied by the Idrissi. The old Asir no longer exists; rather than being a definite section across the middle of the western Penninsula, it has gradually metamorphosed into an elongated coastal strip, like Chile, and the Idrissi's ambition is not to absorb all of Yemen, but to make the coastal strip still longer, thus to hold a whip-hand over the Imam by taking away his coastal territory entirely. The Idrissi people are shouting gleeful war-cries, animated as they are by the sudden access of wealth. It would seem that the British policy with regard to the Idrissi is unlikely to be more felicitous than their mistaken policy regarding ex-King

Hussein of Hedjaz. Even as the Wahhabite conqueror drove out
the British Hachemite protege in the north, so the Imam desires
to drive out the lesser protege in the south. And even as
Great Britain, making a virtue of necessity, recognized and
treated with Ibn Saud, the hope remains that Great Britain may
eventually come to some accord with the Imam, albeit at the
expense of the Idrissi. This seems to be the only way to prevent
war in the Penninsula. On the one hand, the British do not
want to take an active part in Arabian internal politics, yet
on the other, their two outstanding war-time errors have forced
them to take a part, and may yet force them to take a greater
part in Arabian affairs, unless they adopt a new policy and
cease to support such forlorn hopes as the Idrissi. It was with
understanding and feeling that an English acquaintance of the
writer once remarked: "It does seem that as far as Arabia is
concerned, our Government showed an extraordinary propensity
to back the wrong horse."

The Farsan oil concession to a British company merely
means that Great Britain has obtained virtual possession of
another Red Sea island, essentially purchased from the
impecunious Idrissi. If, as time goes on, the Imam should
realize his ambition of driving the Idrissi out, he will find
Great Britain firmly in possession of Farsan, and perhaps then
some arrangement may be made in the interest of future Arabian
tranquillity, a thing much to be desired, but rather too
Utopian to be expected.

There is nothing remarkable in the statement of
the Jeddah correspondent of the paper quoted, that "boring
operations were at once started in consequence of which by
the end of November oil had been found!" since it is not unlikely that oil had been found several thousand years before.

However, preparations have undoubtedly been made for drilling, which by this time is presumably under way, although there is no confirmatory news regarding it.

Some Englishmen have expressed the opinion that the British have "let the Idrissi down" by refusing to fight his battles for him and permitting the Imam to capture Hodeidah as well as generous slices of the Asir Tihama. It were better, perhaps to "let him down" still further, than to keep alive for years to come the spirit of war and hatred and rivalry which is certain to exist between the Idrissi and the Imam as long they both endure. Whatever happens, the odds are still in favor of the Imam, not only because he is a strong ruler, but because Nature itself is his strongest ally.

Oil was probably the ultimate motive for the Anglo-Idrissi treaty of 1917, which recognized Idrissi ownership of Farsan. The oil has finally been purchased legitimately from the Idrissi by British interests, and if the Idrissi insists upon using the purchase money in a pathetic little war against the Imam, he may discover that treaties with great Powers are not necessarily amulets against disaster. British sentiment, as far as I have been able to sound it, is definitely opposed to active interference in Arabian politics and Arabian wars, and this has consistently guided British policy since 1919, except, of course, in the Aden district, where British activity has been in the nature of Empire defense. There is also Ibn Saud to take into account, who might possibly be persuaded to make common cause in Asir. But he has enough to do at present to consolidate his overgrown empire, and even if he deemed the aggression worth the cost in men and money, he is not likely

38

to be generously disposed toward the Idrissi in the division
Idrissi's
of the spoils, and the/~~lxtteris~~ last state would be worse than
his first. His dream of power would evaporate with startling
realism and he would waken to find himself dispossessed not
only of Farsan oil, but of the Farsan Islands as well, without
even a consoling remainder of the latter's purchase price.

Arabian politics are still in a fluid state. It is
impossible to visualize, at this time, a crystallization of
Arabs states in this Penninsula, until the Idrissi, as an
independent ruler, is disposed of, either by expulsion or
absorption, and until Ibn Saud and the Imam, neither of whom
can ever gain a decision over the other, agree upon a
definitive boundary. Again it is seen that much depends
upon the future relations between the Imam and Great Britain.
A happy solution of their differences in turn depends upon
a mutual willingness to make reasonable concessions. The
Imam should concede a sufficient amount of territory around
Aden to render the Protectorate a practicable political entity,
together with commercial and industrial opportunities in Yemen.
The British should refrain from encouraging their adopted
orphan at Jizan to cherish disproportionate territorial
ambitions in the natural Yemen area.

If the perpetuation of little wars in Arabia is
romantic, then truly the Farsan business is "one of the romances
of oil". It all depends upon the point of view. The purchase
of Farsan oil may hasten the inevitable storm and clear the air.

I have the honor to be, Sir,

Your obedient servant,

J. Loder Park,
American Vice Consul.

Enclosures:
1. News item from "The Near
   East & India, 1/13/27
2. Editorial from the same
   issue of the same paper.

NO. 68.

AMERICAN CONSULATE,

BAGHDAD, IRAQ.

CONFIDENTIAL   May 9, 1930.

SUBJECT: OIL CONCESSIONS ON THE ISLAND OF BAHREIN
            AND THE SHORES OF THE PERSIAN GULF.

THE HONORABLE

    THE SECRETARY OF STATE,

        WASHINGTON.

SIR:

I have the honor to refer to despatch No. 400,
dated April 15, 1926, concerning oil concessions in the
Island of Bahrein and the Kingdom of Nejd granted to
Major Frank Holmes for the Eastern and General Syndicate,
Limited, London, and to make further report on that
subject.

On April 28, 1930, Mr. William F. Taylor, General
Superintendent, Producing Department, Foreign Division
of the Standard Oil of California, and Mr. Frederick
Davies, a geologist employed by the same Company, arrived
in Baghdad. Mr. Taylor brought a letter from Sir John
Cadman to the officials of the Iraq Petroleum Company
and visited the fields of that company for a few days.
On May 8th, he and Mr. Davies left for the Island of
Bahrein and will remain there for about six weeks.

Mr. Taylor, whom I had met when he made his annual
inspection trips to Maracaibo, informed me that he and

Mr. Davies had been sent out by their company to inspect oil concessions on the Island of Bahrein on which their company had an option. It appears from his statement of the situation that the Gulf Refining Company obtained an option on these concessions from the Eastern and General Syndicate, but finding that on account of an agreement with the other interests in the Iraq Petroleum Company they could not operate in this territory made arrangements with the Standard Oil Company of California, to take over their option. As I understand the matter, the deal has been arranged and the Standard Oil Company of California is only waiting a favorable report from their representatives to close it.

Mr. Taylor also informed me that the Gulf Refining Company were endeavoring to obtain an oil concession covering the Sheikhdom of Kuwait.

I have the honor to be, Sir,

Your obedient servant,

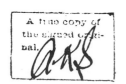

Alexander K. Sloan,
American Consul.

File No. 865.6.
AKS/jnc.

One copy to American Embassy, London;
One copy to American Embassy, Istanbul.

LEGATION OF THE
UNITED STATES OF AMERICA

Bulkeley, August 3, 1931.

August 18 1931.

Dear Mr. Murray:

Mr. K.S. Twitchell, a mining engineer of New
York City who has spent the last two or three years in
the Hedjaz building roads and water systems and making
reconnaissance oil and mineral surveys - being financed
by Mr. Charles R. Crane to carry on this work in the
interest of the Hedjaz people, called at the Legation
on Wednesday, July 29th, on his way to the United States.
His mission to the States at this time is for the purpose of employing a half dozen oil and mining experts
for the Hedjaz Government for a period of three years
(as I remember) to carry on a more or less detailed
survey for oil and minerals, particularly gold.   Mr.
Twitchell carries with him letters from the Finance
Minister of the Hedjaz as well as a cheque from the
same source for seven hundred pounds sterling to cover
the travelling expenses of the said experts to the Hedjaz.
He also carries authorization from the Hedjaz Government
to acquire certain machinery to be used in mining for
oil and for gold.   In fact he seems to have won the

Wallace Murray, Esquire,
        Chief of the Division of Near Eastern Affairs,
        Washington, D.C., U. S. A.

FILED SEP 9 1931

890F.63A/7

2.

complete confidence of the Hedjaz governmental authorities, who are now ready to go forward with a detailed
survey of the mineral resources, including oil, of their
territory; and Twitchell has been assigned the commission
to secure American experts and machines for this purpose.
He has already run on placer gold and oil seepage.

Mr. Twitchell spent a couple of days with Mr.
Dickinson and Mr. Chesbrough, the Commercial Attachees
at Cairo, prior to coming to Alexandria, and Mr. Dickinson
gave him a letter to the Commerce Department. Both
Dickinson and Chesbrough are here at the Legation to-day
and I have talked the matter over with them personally.
They are convinced of the absolute authenticity of all
that Twitchell is claiming for the Hedjaz, and of the
authority which has been invested in him to procure men
and equipment to go forward with the above mentioned
survey.

Twitchell impresses all of us as a genuine man
and thoroughly imbued with the desire to render service
to the Hedjaz people. He is not drawing a salary from
the Government, but from Mr. Crane. He is desirous of
obtaining this equipment on the best terms possible. He
fears, however, that American concerns will be sorely
lacking in knowledge of the Hedjaz Government and will
hesitate to do business except for cash unless they are
convinced that there is a place in the world known as
the Hedjaz and that it seems to have at this time a sta-
ple government under a competent ruler. He will, of

3.

course, be able to tell them that our Government has recently recognized that of the Hedjaz.

Twitchell wished me to give him a letter, which he might use, to the effect that the Hedjaz does exist and has a competent king and a stable government capable and willing to honor its obligations, financial and otherwise, which government has recently been recognized by ours. Rather than provide him with such a letter I gave him one of introduction to you. He expects to be in Washington at an early date, when doubtless he will seek a conference.

It is the judgment of all of us here that Twitchell is doing an excellent piece of work in the Hedjaz, and that there is a possibility, through this survey which will be under his direction, of opening up first class contacts with the Hedjaz Government which will eventually develop into real business opportunities. I am sure we should encourage him as far as is consistent with the rules and regulations of the Department of State. You will know how far you can go after talking to him and examining his documents.

Sincerely yours,

W. M. Jardine.

August 18, 1931.

Dear Mr. Jardine:

I wish to thank you for your letter of August 3, 1931, regarding the interesting work which Mr. K. S. Twitchell, a mining engineer of New York City, has been doing in the Hejaz on the bounty of Mr. Charles R. Crane.

I shall be much interested in meeting Mr. Twitchell if and when he comes to Washington and calls at the Department. We are of course anxious to do anything that we can to develop our foreign trade, and if there is a possibility in this direction with the Hejaz we shall be only too happy to give Mr. Twitchell every proper assistance.

I am glad that you did not meet Mr. Twitchell's request that you give him a letter stating among other things that the Hejaz Government is "capable and willing to honor its obligations." His request was quite out of order and it would, furthermore, be difficult for any of us to commit ourselves in writing in the above sense

The Honorable
        William M. Jardine,
                American Minister,
                        Cairo.

- 2 -

regarding almost any Near Eastern country.   Responsibility
for foreign investments must in the last analysis rest upon
the investors themselves who should, through competent
agents, investigate the situation on the spot and negotiate
sound agreements with the competent authorities.

I wish to take this occasion to compliment you on the
form of report which you are now submitting in place of the
former review of the Egyptian press.   It is a much more
useful contribution from every point of view than the old
review.   I have no suggestions at this moment as to any
modification of the form of despatch which you have adopted
but I am sure that as time goes on new ideas in this connection may occur to you which you may care to put into operation.   Any suggestions that you may ever have to make along
such lines will always be most welcome to the Division.

With best wishes, believe me

Sincerely yours,

Wallace Murray

NE/WSM/GC

Aug. 18. 1931.

PM RECD

LEGATION OF THE
UNITED STATES OF AMERICA
Baghdad, Iraq.   February 6, 1932.

MAR 1 32

Diplomatic Series No. 120.

890F.63A

FOR DISTRIBUTION - CHECK   Yes   No
To the Field
In U. S. A.

i MAR 8 - 1932

The Honorable,

    The Secretary of State,

        Washington, D. C.

Sir:

    I have the honor to transmit to the Department some
information recently received from Bahrein which may be
of interest.

    Dr. Luis J. Dame, an American missionary stationed
at Bahrein, informed me in a letter dated January 27th
that about the first of the year a Mr. Twitchel suddenly
and unexpectedly arrived in Bahrein from the mainland.
He added that Mr. Twitchel is reported to be an expert
mining engineer in the employ of Mr. Charles R. Crane

and loaned by that gentleman to King Ibn Sa'oud to explore and search his domain for natural resources. Dr.
Dame had several conversations with Mr. Twitchel who
informed him that immediately prior to coming to Bahrein
he had spent some time at Hassa, at Qatif, and at
Jubail and believes that there is mineral in the Hejaz
and oil in the Qatif and Jubail areas. Dr. Dame was
informed that Mr. Twitchel makes his reports to King
Ibn Sa'oud only and not to any financial group or
corporation. He adds that Mr. Twitchel after spending
some two or three months in further prospecting expects
to return to Jeddah where his wife is awaiting him.

Respectfully yours,

Alexander K. Sloan.

TELEGRAM RECEIVED

REP

FROM San Francisco, California

October 25, 1932

Rec'd 26th, 12:18 a.m.

The Honorable Secretary of State,

Washington.

Confidential. Standard Oil Company of California contemplates entering into a contract with Ibn Saud to search for and produce petroleum if found in commerce quantities in the Persian Gulf coastal regions of Hasa. Has United States a treaty with King of Arabia? What protection could we expect in case of disorders in Arabia or in case the present government is overthrown and its successor were disposed to break our contract without just cause? Could legal aspects of controversy be adjudicated in any of the established international tribunals or elsewhere outside of Arabia or would we be wholly at mercy of arbitrary sovereign? Is there any likelihood that the United States Government may establish diplomatic relations with Ibn Saud as Great Britain, Holland and some other governments have done? Please telegraph answer at your earliest convenience collect.

Francis B. Loomis

HPD

890F.6363 STANDARD OIL CO./2

TELEGRAM SENT

PREPARING OFFICE
WILL INDICATE WHETHER

Collect **X**

Charge Department

Charge to
$

288 collect DL

TO BE TRANSMITTED
CONFIDENTIAL CODE
NONCONFIDENTIAL CODE
PLAIN

Department of State

Washington,

October 26, 1932.

The Honorable

Francis B. Loomis,

225 Bush Street,

San Francisco, California.

note
124.90f
125.0090f
390f.11

CONFIDENTIAL

This Government has no treaty with Ibn Saud but it
has agreed to negotiate a treaty of commerce and navigation.
Meanwhile, in an exchange of notes which is now in the
process of negotiation provision is made that American
nationals in Saudi Arabia shall enjoy the fullest protection
of the laws and authorities of the country and that they
shall not be treated in regard to their persons, property,
rights and interests in any manner less favorable than the
nationals of any other country. Provision is also made for
most-favored-nation treatment in respect of import, export
and other duties and charges affecting commerce and navigation
as well as in respect of transit, warehousing and other
facilities. As far as the Department is aware the Arabian
Government has concluded no detailed treaties or agreements
specifying exact rights and privileges in such matters.

The Department is unable to indicate in advance the

Enciphered by _____

Sent by operator _____ M., _____, 19___

Index Bu.—No. 50.

PREPARING OFFICE
WILL INDICATE WHETHER

Collect

Charge Department
or

Charge to
$

TELEGRAM SENT

Department of State

Washington,

TO BE TRANSMITTED
CONFIDENTIAL CODE
NONCONFIDENTIAL CODE
PLAIN

- 2 -

nature of the protection, if any, which it could accord in the event of the contingencies to which you refer, but you will doubtless appreciate   the possible difficulty of insuring effective protection for American interests.

The Department is not aware that Ibn Saud has entered into any arrangements by which controversies arising in his territory could be adjudicated in any established international tribunal or elsewhere outside of Arabia.

Although this Government has recognized the Arabian Kingdom and is in diplomatic relations with it through the respective representatives of the two Governments in London, it is not contemplated that this Government will establish diplomatic or consular representation at Jeddah in the near future. The eventual establishment of such representation will, of course, depend upon the character and growth of American interests in the Arabian Kingdom.

NE PHA/LM

890F.6363 Standard Oil Co.

DEPARTMENT OF STATE
DIVISION OF
COMMUNICATIONS & RECORDS

OCT 27 1932.

Enciphered by ....

Sent by operator .... M., ... 19....,

Index Bu.—No. 50.

DEPARTMENT OF STATE
—
DIVISION OF NEAR EASTERN AFFAIRS

CONFIDENTIAL   November 1, 1932

Karl?

MEMORANDUM OF CONVERSATION WITH MR. KENNETH TWITCHELL REGARDING THE KINGDOM OF SAUDI ARABIA

Mr. Kenneth Twitchell, accompanied by his wife, called to relate some of his experiences in the Hajaz and Nejd (now known as the Kingdom of Saudi Arabia). In the employ of Mr. Charles R. Crane of Chicago, he had spent some time in various parts of Saudi Arabia, basing on the Red Sea port of Jedda, and had traveled overland to the Persian Gulf by motor caravan. On this journey he had skirted Mecca, visiting Taif, and, avoiding Riyadh, had met King Ibn Saud at some distance from the latter city. He had then continued to Hufuf and to the coast of El Hasa, where he had visited Bahrein and the neighboring islands of the Persian Gulf.

Mr. Twitchell, a geologist by profession, stated that the object of his explorations was three-fold: to search for petroleum; to prospect for gold and other minerals; and to investigate the opportunities for engineering and public utility projects. He said that while he continued to preserve his connection with Mr. Crane, it was no longer of a financial nature and that his plans now were to attempt to interest responsible American firms in the possibilities of Saudi Arabia along the above lines. He mentioned Mr. Guy Stevens of the Gulf Exploration Company as one who had already indicated an interest in the gold and oil of that area.

890F.6363/10

FILED
NOV 7 1932

DEPARTMENT OF STATE
—
DIVISION OF NEAR EASTERN AFFAIRS

-2-

In Mr. Twitchell's opinion, the most promising oil fields lay in El Hasa, to the south of Kuwait, for which the town of Hufuf would be a logical base of operations. The gold region lay to the south of Medina, where ancient mines existed; but there was a strong probability that both oil and gold, as well as other minerals, might be found in other parts of the Kingdom, such as the northern Red Sea littoral, should a scientific survey be undertaken. The most important work of an engineering character would be the construction of roads, one stretch of which had already been laid out by Mr. Twitchell through the mountainous district near the seacoast, while public utility projects would include lighting, irrigation, and power plants for cities such as Jedda or Medina. I asked whether Saudi Arabia was in a position to spend any money on such projects, to which Mr. Twitchell answered that appropriations for this sort of work would have to come out of revenue derived from whatever mineral development took place.

Mr. Twitchell said that the present was an excellent time for American interests to enter the scene in Saudi Arabia. King Ibn Saud, he asserted, was disposed to be very friendly to the United States and was hopeful that Americans, who had no political ax to grind, would become interested in the

exploitation of the natural resources of his Kingdom. The
pilgrimage business, from which Saudi Arabia derives most
of its revenue, has been seriously hit by the depression,
and the revenue that might be expected from oil or other
mineral development would be especially welcome at this time.

Mr. Twitchell urged that the Department should now
consider the advisability of establishing diplomatic or
consular representation in Saudi Arabia, saying that there
was just as much reason to have such representation in
Saudi Arabia as in Ethiopia, and that Jedda would be the
natural place to establish a legation or consulate. It was
apparent that Mr. Twitchell believed that the presence there
of an American diplomatic or consular officer would assist
him in his efforts to bring American enterprise to Saudi
Arabia and that he hoped that the flag in this case might
precede trade. I replied that while we might eventually have
to take under consideration the question of establishing
direct diplomatic relations with Saudi Arabia, the absence of
any American interests in that Kingdom at present would, for
the time being, probably prevent us from acting along the
lines he suggested. I said that we would of course be greatly
interested in watching developments and that as soon as existing American interests appeared to warrant it, we would go

into the matter further, at which time I said I hoped we would have the benefit of his researches in that country. Mr. Twitchell said that his future movements were uncertain, but that he would always be glad to assist us in any way he could.

I asked Mr. Twitchell regarding conditions in Jedda, and he replied that as far as climate was concerned, it was not only very warm but very humid. After a heavy rain vegetation appeared which soon dried up in the heat, but this showed that irrigation would be successful in many parts of the country. He said that in most places, including the desert route he followed from the Red Sea to the Persian Gulf, it was entirely possible to secure artesian well water and that pumping could readily be effected by windmills. Although facilities were still primitive at Jedda, he said that Europeans, except their children, found it quite feasible to stand the climate, and that if it were decided to open a legation or consulate, the local authorities would be more than glad to place the best available building at our disposal. The foreign colony at present consists of 45 persons, mostly British, but including also Dutch, French, Italian, Persian, Iraqi and, in increasing number, Soviet representatives.

DEPARTMENT OF STATE

DIVISION OF NEAR EASTERN AFFAIRS

-5-

Of these, the Dutch were the most friendly, while the British, he said, would be sure to look with suspicion and disfavor on the entrance of American interests.

Mr. Twitchell impressed me as a man of obvious integrity and sincerity. He has a fund of valuable knowledge about Saudi Arabia and a collection of photographs which he is willing to show the Department at any time. His wife seemed to be an intelligent woman, who took an active interest in her husband's affairs.

H. S. Villard

DEPARTMENT OF STATE
———
DIVISION OF NEAR EASTERN AFFAIRS

December 1, 1932.

CONVERSATION WITH MR. FRANCIS B. LOOMIS
REGARDING THE INTEREST OF THE STANDARD OIL
COMPANY OF CALIFORNIA IN EL HASA.

Mr. Loomis called on me on November 16 to inquire whether
the British have any control over El Hasa, a portion of Ibn Saud's
realm bordering on the Persian Gulf, and whether there would be
any objection to negotiating directly with Ibn Saud with a view
to obtaining a concession to prospect for oil in that region.

I told Mr. Loomis that as far as the Department is aware
the British have no control over El Hasa and that Ibn Saud would
appear to be entirely free to grant a concession in that area
should he please to do so.   Mr. Loomis then stated that
Major Frank Holmes, who assisted in obtaining the oil concession
now held by the Standard Oil Company of California in the
Bahrein Islands, had offered to assist that Company in obtaining
the desired concession in El Hasa.   It appears, however, that
the Company does not repose complete confidence in Major Holmes
and does not believe that Major Holmes has the influence with
Ibn Saud which he pretends to have.   Mr. Loomis stated that
on one occasion when Holmes had gone to the Nejd to see Ibn Saud
about this matter Ibn Saud had refused to receive him.
Mr. Loomis thought this resulted from the fact that Holmes had

earlier negotiated with Ibn Saud on behalf of the Eastern
General Syndicate and that the promises then given were not
fulfilled.   Mr. Loomis mentioned the names of St. John Philby
and Mr. K. S. Twitchell as possible agents of his Company in
these negotiations.   He said he knew Philby very well and
was impressed by him. He does not know Twitchell personally,
although his Company has been in correspondence with him.   I
remarked that this Division had had several conferences with
Mr. Twitchell and that he had made a very favorable impression
on us. I stated that everything else being equal it would
appear to be desirable for the Company to entrust any eventual
negotiations that it might have with Ibn Saud to an American
rather than to a foreigner. I told Mr. Loomis that I did
not wish him to understand that we were vouching for Mr. Twitchell
or that we did not have confidence in Mr. Philby; that I merely
felt that in matters of this kind where concessions are being
sought by an American company the American nationality of the
negotiator was of no little importance.

Mr. Loomis then told me that his Company was going
forward with its work in the Bahrein Islands but that
the British were placing petty obstacles in its way since
the discovery of oil there.   He referred also to the

DEPARTMENT OF STATE

———

DIVISION OF NEAR EASTERN AFFAIRS

- 2 -

difficulties which the Gulf Oil is having in its endeavors
to obtain a concession in Kuwait and seemed to be almost
pleased at these difficulties.

Wallace Murray

WSM/GC

DEPARTMENT OF STATE
DIVISION OF NEAR EASTERN AFFAIRS

December 15, 1932.

Mr. Francis B. Loomis of the Standard Oil Company of California called today, accompanied by Mr. Kenneth S. Twitchell. Loomis said that he expected that Mr. Twitchell would leave during the first part of January for Jeddah where he would enter into negotiations with the Arabian Government regarding a concession for the development of petroleum resources in that Kingdom. Mr. Loomis said that Mr. Twitchell was of the opinion that it would be desirable for him to have some sort of an official document indicating that the Standard Oil Company of California was an American corporation of good reputation, and he inquired whether it would be possible to obtain such a document from the Department. He was advised, in reply, that probably the proper procedure to follow in obtaining such a document would be to request the authorities of the State of Delaware, in which state the company is incorporated, to issue a certificate indicating the American character of the company; the Department of State would then be in a position to certify that this document is under the seal of the State of Delaware and the papers would then be in proper form for use in Arabia.

Mr. Twitchell stated that we might be interested in knowing that the John Monks Company are taking an interest in the possibility of constructing roads and establishing water supplies

890F.6363 STANDARD OIL CO./4

890F.6363
Standard
Oil Co.

note
890F.154

in Saudi Arabia.   This proposition is still in a formative
stage but Mr. Twitchell said he thought that in view of the
low cost of construction in Arabia it might be possible for
the Monks Company to make some arrangements with the Arabian
Government.   Asked how this proposed construction was to be
paid for, Mr. Twitchell said the Monks Company had in mind
requesting the Arabian Government to collect a special tax
the proceeds of which would be used to defray the expenses of
construction.

In leaving Mr. Loomis stated that now that their expedition
in Bahrein had discovered oil, his company is having certain
difficulties in inducing the Colonial Office to agree to the
terms of the contract covering the Bahrein operations.   He said
that these negotiations had first appeared to be progressing
favorably but that as soon as oil was found the company encountered difficulties.   Mr. Loomis added that he had recently been told by the Standard Oil Company of New York that the
Anglo-Persian Oil Company had a petroleum concession covering
the exploration of petroleum resources in Qatar.   It was said
that Sir John Cadman had proposed to retain this concession
for the benefit of the A.P.O.C. but that the other groups,
particularly, the American group, in the Iraq Petroleum Company

had finally obliged Sir John Cadman to turn over this concession to the I.P.C. in accordance with the terms of the
self-denying ordinance set forth in the agreement which was
signed between the constituent members of the I.P.C.

Mr. Loomis also stated that he had understood that the
Gulf Oil Company was encountering difficulties in connection
with the proposed concession in Kuwait.   He added that he
was not at all surprised at this development because when
he was in London several months ago Sir John Cadman told
him that the A.P.O.C. intended to obtain a concession in
that territory.

890.B.6363
Gulf Oil Corp.

PHA/GC

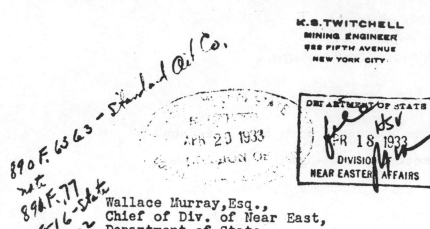

K.S.TWITCHELL
MINING ENGINEER
782 FIFTH AVENUE
NEW YORK CITY

DEPARTMENT OF STATE
R 18 1933
DIVISION
NEAR EASTERN AFFAIRS

Jedda,
Hedjaz,
Saudi-Arabia.

April   1933
March 26,1933.

890F.6363 STANDARD OIL CO./9

Wallace Murray,Esq.,
Chief of Div. of Near East,
Department of State,
Washington, D.C.

Dear Mr.Murray;-

   As you wrote in your last letter to me that you
would be interested in hearing of my negotiations here as well as
matters in general, I am inflicting this letter upon you.

   In the first place negotiations are taking more time
than we expected, but this is charactistic of all countries "east
of Suez" I think, do you not agree ?   The Government has expressed
a most friendly feeling towrds us as well as a decided preference ffor
us over our competitors who are the Iraq Petroleum Co. But all depends upon the amount of money we or the others can make available
to the Government either as a loan or as a payment.

   I am enclosing a statement of a synopsis of two concessions concluded by this Government during the past two months. I
thought this information might possibly be of interest to you. The
Government now fully realizes that its present principle source of
revenue - the Pilgrims - is a very uncertain one, and that a competent development of oil and mines is their very best chance for a
permanent prosperity.   I was informed that they frequently study
my reports made last year regarding the above as well as water development.

   I am hoping that the new Bank will take up the subjects
of roads, water supply for Jedda, and electric power for Jedda,Mecca,
and Medina.   I can do nothing effective till after the oil agreement is reached.

   I expect to visit the mines in the Sudan in which I am
interested after we leave here. Then I may have to make a short trip
to central Iraq before sailing for home.

   When Convenient I shall be glad to hear from you and
to have your views on the present banking crisis and the probabili-
ties of a real sound reorganization.   I shall also be very much
interested to know how the treaty with this Government is progressing
I certainly do appreciate your allowing me to see it when I was in
London.   If I can be of any service to you in any way,here or nearby,
please let me know.

     Yours sincerely, K.S.Twitchell

Synopsis of Concessions signed by the Government of Saudi-
Arabia with the following Companies during the month of March
and February 1933.

RAILWAY.

A railway line is to be co nstruced from Jedda to Mecca for the trans‌
portation of pilgrims.   Construction to be commenced by October
1933 and line to be in operation by March 1935.   Company is to be entirely Muslim and capital is being raised in India.
Government is to receive a loan of ten lkhs of rupees payable
in monthly lots of two lakhs each and payments to begin October 1933. This
loan is to be repaid by the Government out of its revenues from the Railway
receipts of which it is to receive 50% (being 50% of the gross receipts).
The repayment is to be 5% of the Goverments share till it is repaid.(Of
course there are no interest charges, as interest is not allowed by the Koran

STATE BANK.

This bank is to loan the Government the sum of 200,000 pounds-
gold- on the day the bank begins to operate which is to be April
1933.   The methods of repayment are not exactly stated as far as can be ascertained, but the Government is to pay all its revenues into the bank so
loan will take the form of -probably - of a reducible credit, as well as a
revolving credit, which will vary according to the Goevrnment's receipts
from its share of the profits in the note issues.   Besides these note
issues the Government has no share in the profits of the Bank, althoughit
has the right to subscribe to one quater of the total capital stock which
to be one million pounds-gold.   The Ex-Khedive of Egypt is taking one half
of the total capital stock and the one quarter remaining is open to public
subscription.   It is understood that the portion of the capital reserved
for the Government has been underwritten by a syndicate which is entirely
or almost entirely British.
The distribution of the profits of the Bank is to be as follows;
45% to shareholders; 25% to reserve;: 20% to special reserve; 2½% to provide scholarships for promising students to go to study in Europe, and 7½%
to the Founders.   This 7½% share is to be divided viz; 30% to the King
30% to the Khedive; 10% to Abdullah Suleiman (the Finance Minister); 10%
to Shadid Bey (the representative of the Khedive) 10% to fees of Directors;
andcthe last 10% be be at the disposal of the King for use in making re-
wards for services of especial merit, as he may decide.
The notes to be issued are to be legal tender only after they
have been established on their merits in the foreign markets.
The Bank is to have some sort of prior right or lien on every
concession granted by the Government but this is not yet clearly stated
nad will not have any effect till after the Bank begins to function, and wll
have no bearing on any concessions granted before that time.   It would seem
that it would be to the interest of the Bank to further all lgitimate concessions and take a small capital interest in them.
This bank concession has not yet been officially published
but the railway one has been in the Government weekly newspare at Mecca.

NO. 140

AMERICAN CONSULATE

Cairo, Egypt, April 22, 1933

STRICTLY CONFIDENTIAL

MAY 17 1933

SUBJECT: Negotiations of the Standard Oil Company of
California for an Oil Concession in Saudi Arabia.

THE HONORABLE

THE SECRETARY OF STATE

WASHINGTON

FOR DISTRIBUTION - CHECK   Yes   No

To the Field

In U. S. A.

SIR:

I have the honor to report that Mr. M. E. Lombardi,
a director of the Standard Oil Company of California, and
Mr. Lloyd N. Hamilton an official of the same company,
were recently in Cairo, and to submit, as of possible
interest to the Department, certain information concerning
the negotiations of the above-mentioned company for an oil
concession in the Kingdom of Saudi Arabia.

Mr. Hamilton went to Jidda some two or three months
ago, accompanied by Mr. K. S. Twitchell who formerly spent
some time studying the mineral and water resources of Saudi
Arabia while in the employ of Mr. Charles R. Crane. He has
opened negotiations for an exploring and exploiting concession, and it is understood that he has been assisted to
some extent in these negotiations by Mr. H. St. John Philby,
the well-known Arabian traveler.

In the meantime Mr. Lombardi proceeded via Baghdad to
Bahrein Islands to inspect the operations being carried on
there by the Bahrein Petroleum Company, and later touched
at Jidda whence he was accompanied to Cairo by Mr. Hamilton

for the purpose of discussing the progress of the negotiations.
They were joined in Cairo by Major Holmes, an Englishman
now in the employ of the Bahrein Petroleum Company, and
who was instrumental in securing the concession now being
worked by that company in Bahrein.

The exact limits of the area for which the Standard
Oil Company desires to obtain an exploring concession are
not known to me. However, it is understood to include
principally the Hassa district of the Nejd. The reasons
for assuming that valuable oil resources are to be found
in this district are based upon Mr. Twitchell's preliminary
geological survey; the finding of oil in Bahrein, the
knowledge that the oil bearing strata of Southern Persia
extend toward the Arabian side of the Persian Gulf; and
the discovery of the presence of oil in shallow wells
already existing near the coast on the Arabian side of
the Gulf.

Incidentally, Mr. Lombardi believes that water in
quantities sufficient for limited agricultural development could be obtained by drilling water wells in the Hassa
district.

It appears that Ibn Saud desires very much to negotiate
a foreign loan, and that he has offered to grant an oil
concession to the Standard Oil Company of California in
return for an advance of £ 100,000. The Company is not
willing to advance such a large sum without the opportunity of first carrying out exploring operations, and has
in turn offered a smaller sum for an exploring concession
with a further amount to be advanced later in the event
an exploiting concession is obtained. The Company is
naturally mindful of the fact that political disturbances

would undoubtedly occur in the event of Ibn Saud's death in the near future.

In the meantime the Iraq Petroleum Company is reported to be endeavoring to obtain an oil concession. Two employees of that Company, Mr. Shaw, an American geologist, and Mr. Longrigg, an Englishman formerly attached to the Ministry of Finance of the Iraq Government, are understood to be in Saudi Arabia at the present time.

Ibn Saud is said to have admitted that he prefers to deal with the Standard Oil Company of California, the reason being that the United States would not be so likely to interfere in the event of internal disturbance occurring as would be the case if the interests of the nationals of certain other governments were involved.

Mr. Lombardi has left Egypt for London en route to the United States, while Mr. Hamilton has returned to Jidda to continue negotiations. Should he have occasion to visit Cairo again, an effort will be made to ascertain whether further progress has been made.

This despatch is based upon a conversation had by Vice Consul Robert Y. Brown with Mr. Lombardi and Mr. Hamilton. Mr. Charles E. Dickerson, Commercial Attache in Cairo was also present at the time and has had several other interviews with both Mr. Lombardi and Mr. Hamilton. It is understood that Mr. Dickerson has reported in detail to the Department of Commerce in a confidential letter dated April 15, 1933, a copy of which could be obtained from that Department.

Respectfully yours,

Gordon P. Merriam,
American Consul.

DISTRIBUTION:

Original and four copies to the Department.
One Copy to American Consulate General Alexandria.
One Copy to American Legation, Cairo.
One Copy to American Legation, Baghdad.

File No. 863.6

RYB/am.

4 Carbon Copies
Received F.P.___Z.E.C.
1 copy in L.G.R.-L.E.C.

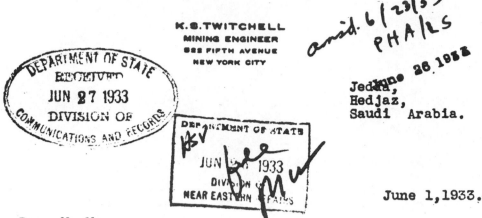

K.S.TWITCHELL
MINING ENGINEER
522 FIFTH AVENUE
NEW YORK CITY

ansd. 6/23/33
PHA/LS

Jedda,
Hedjaz,
Saudi Arabia.

June 26.1933

June 1,1933.

890F.6363 STANDARD OIL CO./13

Dear Mr.Murray;

Your good letter dated April 19 was received May 7.   I am glad that the information I sent you was of interest.   I was very glad to receive your statement re the progress of the treaty you are negotiating with this country through the London Embassy.

The occasion of my inflicting this letter upon you is to give the information that the Saudi Arab Government through its Minister of Finance, Sheik Abdulla Suleiman Hamdan signed a concession for the exploration and exploitation of the oil resources of eastern Saudi Arabia with L.N.Hamilton representing the Standard Oil Company of California on May 29,1933 at Jedda.

Mr.Hamilton has left for London and Cairo. The documents are being sent to SanFrancisco for ratification there. When I notify this Government this has been done the King will issue a decree and the concession will be published in the official newspaper at Mecca thereupon the concession will become effective.   Until the publication date I am not at liberty to state the terms of this concession. I hope that this concession will be a great step towards increasing the prosperity of the country.   Also I hope it will mean official representation by our own Government.

Yours sincerely,

K S Twitchell

No. 159

AMERICAN CONSULATE
Cairo, Egypt, June 10, 1933.

STRICTLY CONFIDENTIAL

SUBJECT: Standard Oil Company of California obtains Oil

Concession from the Government of Saudi Arabia.

FOR DISTRIBUTION - CHECK   Yes   No

In the Field

In U. S. A.

THE HONORABLE

THE SECRETARY OF STATE

WASHINGTON

SIR:

I have the honor to refer to my confidential despatch No. 140 of April 22, 1933, entitled "Negotiations of the Standard Oil Company of California for an Oil Concession in Saudi Arabia", File No. 863.6, and to report that an agreement for an oil concession was signed at Jidda on May 29, 1933, by Mr. Lloyd N. Hamilton, representing the Standard Oil Company of California, and representatives of the Government of Saudi Arabia.

The Concession becomes effective upon its being ratified or approved by the Company. The Company has 15 days from the date the documents are received in San Francisco, California, within which to ratify or reject the concession, and it is understood that the pertinent documents were forwarded by mail from Egypt to the Company's San Francisco office by Mr. Hamilton on or about June 7, 1933.

This office is indebted to Mr. Charles E. Dickerson, American Commercial Attache, Cairo, for its original

- 2 -

contact with Mr. Hamilton, and for having made available
to the Consulate a summary of the concession, as dictated
by Mr. Hamilton, which reads as follows:

"1. Concession gives exclusive oil exploration and
exploitation rights covering all of eastern Saudi Arabia from
Persian Gulf coast westward to the westerly edge of the
Dahna and from the northern boundary to the southern
boundary of Saudi Arabia. This area is referred to as
the "exclusive area". To complete the description of the
westerly side of this exclusive area a straight line is
projected north 30 degrees west from the northern end of
the westerly edge of the Dahna to the northerly border
and similarly south 30 degrees east from the southern
end of the westerly edge of the Dahna to the southern
boundary of Saudi Arabia.

"The Company is also given a preference right to
acquire an oil concession covering the balance of the
eastern part of Saudi Arabia as far to the west of the
exclusive area as the sedimentary - igneous contact.
The preference right also includes such rights as the
Government may have in the so-called Neutral Zone to
the south of Kuwait.

"2. The Company has 15 days from the date the documents
are received in San Francisco, California, within which
to ratify or to reject the concession. The effective
date of the concession is the date of its ratification
by the Company in San Francisco.

"3. Upon the ratification of the concession the
company is to loan the Government 30,000 pounds gold,
or its equivalent in sterling, at the current rate of
exchange when the payment is made.

"4. If the concession is not relinquished sooner,
the Company is to make a further loan, 18 months from
the effective date, of 20,000 pounds gold or its equivalent.

"5. The annual rental, payable in advance commencing
with the effective date is 5,000 pounds gold, or its
equivalent. After the discovery of oil in commercial
quantities no further annual rentals are due.

"6. Geological field work is to be commenced not
later than September 30, 1933.

"7. Geological work is to be continued diligently
until a suitable structure has been discovered, or the
contract terminated.

"8. Drilling operations are to commence as soon as
a suitable structure has been found (but in no event later
than September 30, 1936) and are to be continued until
oil has been discovered in commercial quantities or until
the contract has been terminated.

"9. Upon the discovery of oil in commercial quantities the Company is to advance the Government on account of future royalties 50,000 pounds gold, or its equivalent, and similarly another 50,000 pounds gold or its equivalent is to be advanced the Government one year after the date of commercial discovery. Also upon commercial discovery the Company is to continue drilling operations with at least two strings of tools until the proven area has been drilled up, or until the contract has been terminated.

"10. The royalty rate is four shillings gold, or its equivalent, per ton, or at the option of the Company it is $1.00 per ton, provided, however, that if the dollar drops below the equivalent of $1.10 for four shillings gold, the difference shall be added to the royalty rate of $1.00. Thus, for example, if it costs $1.14 for four shillings gold the royalty rate would be $1.04 per ton. Royalty is payable semi-annually.

"If the Company sells any natural gas it must also pay the Government one-eighth of the proceeds of the sale. The Company, however, is under no obligation to produce or sell gas, or to pay royalty on gas used in its operations. Nor is the Company required to pay royalty on oil used in its operations or on oil required to manufacture the gasolene and kerosene to be delivered free to the Government each year.

"11. After commercial discovery the Company is to erect a plant for manufacturing sufficient gasolene and kerosene to meet the ordinary requirement of the Government. Furthermore, the Company is to offer the Government free each year 200,000 American gallons of gasolene and 100,000 American gallons of kerosene.

"12. The initial loan of 30,000 pounds gold, or its equivalent in sterling, and the second loan of 20,000 pounds gold, or its equivalent, are to be recovered by the Company by way of deductions from one-half of the royalties due to the Government. If not so recovered these sums are to be repaid the Company by the Government in four annual instalments, the first of which will be due one year after the termination of the contract.

"The two advances of 50,000 pounds gold, or the equivalent, are also to be recovered by the Company by way of deductions from one-half of the royalties due the Government, but they are not recoverable otherwise.

"13. If the initial payment (comprising the loan of 30,000 pounds and the first annual rental of 5,000 pounds) is not made in gold, it will be made in the equivalent thereof in sterling at the current rate of exchange when the payment is made. This payment is to be made within 15 days of the effective date to a correspondent, in New York or in London, of the Dutch bank in Jeddah for transmission to the Dutch Bank in Jeddah, which will then pay the sum to the Government.

"The subsequent payments due in gold or its equivalent may be paid in dollars or in sterling at the average rate of exchange over a period of three months preceding due date of payment. The Government is to designate a bank in the United States, England or Holland to which the subsequent payments may be made. The Government also has

- 4 -

a right to designate a bank in Saudi Arabia provided that
such bank has a correspondent in the United States, England,
or Holland through which the payments may be made.

"In all cases, the equivalent of the gold pound is to
be based on the value of the gold pound according to its
weight and fineness at the time of the payments.

"14. Although the English and Arabic texts have equal
validity the English text is to govern in the case of any
divergence, as far as the Company's obligations are
concerned.

"15. The Company and enterprise are free of all taxes,
although this privilege of course does not extend to the
personal requirements of the employees nor does it extend
to the sale of products within the country.

"16. Disputes are to be settled by arbitration.

"17. The Company may terminate the contract at any
time by giving the Government an advance notice of one
month."

In addition to the terms outlined in the summary set
forth above, it is understood that the concession stipulates
that the management of the Company's operations in Saudi
Arabia must be under the direction of American citizens.
It is further understood that this stipulation applies to
any company to which the Standard Oil Company of California
might eventually transfer its concession. This provision
is of particular interest in view of the fact that the
Bahrein Petroleum Company is required to negotiate with
the Native Government through the medium of a British
subject in connection with its operations in the Bahrein
Islands.

In my despatch No. 140 of April 22, 1933, it was
stated that the Iraq Petroleum Company was reported to
be seeking an oil concession in Saudi Arabia, and that
Mr. Longrigg, an Englishman formerly attached to the
Iraq Ministry of Finance, was then in Saudi Arabia in
the interest of the Iraq Petroleum Company. Mr. Hamilton

reports that Mr. Longrigg left Jidda for London on May
27, 1933, the day before the signing of the Standard Oil
Company of California's concession. Mr. Hamilton is of
the opinion that British interests will be very much
displeased that an American Company has secured an oil
concession in Saudi Arabia, and that renewed and strong
opposition may be expected as regards the efforts being
made by an American Company to obtain an oil concession
in Koweit.

The writer is of the belief, having in mind the
terms of oil concessions granted to foreign companies
by the Governments of Iraq and Persia, that the terms
of the concession granted by Saudi Arabia to the Standard
Oil Company of California are extremely favorable from
the point of view of the Company's interests. It would
appear that the only risk being taken by the Company
has to do with the stability of the present regime of
Government in Saudi Arabia.

It would further appear that the granting of this
oil concession by the Government of Saudi Arabia is of
unusual interest in that it is believed to be the first
concession of any kind granted to a foreign (non-Moslem)
company by Ibn Saud, and it may prove to be the opening
wedge towards the admission of foreign capital and enterprise with a view to the exploitation of the mineral and
commercial resources of the Arabian peninsular proper.

It is understood that a copy of the complete English
text of the concession granted to the Standard Oil Company
of California will be made available shortly to the
American Legation at Cairo, and the Department will
doubtlessly receive a copy thereof through the medium of
that office. Inasmuch as the Company may not have had an

opportunity to take final action in approving or rejecting
the concession by the time this despatch reaches the
Department, it is respectfully requested that the information contained herein be treated as strictly confidential

Respectfully yours,

Gordon P. Merriam,
American Consul.

File No. 863.6

RYB/am.

4 Carbon Copies
Received

DISTRIBUTION:

Original and four copies to the Department;
1 copy to the American Consulate General, Alexandria;
1 copy to the American Legation, Cairo;
1 copy to the American Legation, Baghdad.

AMERICAN CONSULATE

Cairo, Egypt, June 19, 1933.

STRICTLY CONFIDENTIAL

SUBJECT: Transmitting Agreement Covering Oil Concession
of the Standard Oil Company of California in
Saudi Arabia.

JUL 29 1933

THE HONORABLE

THE SECRETARY OF STATE

WASHINGTON

TREATY DIVISION
JUL 27 1933
DEPARTMENT OF STATE

890F.6363 STANDARD OIL CO./16

SIR:

I have the honor to refer to my confidential despatch
No. 159 of June 10, 1933, entitled "Standard Oil Company
of California Obtains Oil Concession from the Government
of Saudi Arabia", File No. 863.6, and to transmit herewith
a copy of the complete English text of the agreement
discussed in that despatch.

There is also enclosed a copy of a supplementary
agreement by the provisions of which the Company is
accorded preference rights to oil concessions covering
certain other areas in Saudi Arabia, not included in the
exclusive area defined by the principal agreement, and
also in the so-called Neutral Zone, with respect to the
rights of Saudi Arabia in that area. This supplementary
agreement is also designed to regulate the use of aeroplanes
by the Company within Saudi Arabia.

Although article 37 of the principal agreement pro-
vides for publication of that agreement in Jidda, subject
to and subsequent to its ratification by the Company, it

- 2 -

is understood to be probable that the full text may not be published.

Respectfully yours,

Gordon P. Merriam,
American Consul.

2 Enclosures:

1. Copy of Agreement;
2. Copy of Supplementary Agreement.

File No. 863.6

RYB/am.

4 Carbon Copies
Received _____

1 Copy in DC

DISTRIBUTION:
Original and four copies to the Department;
One copy to American Consulate General, Alexandria;
One Copy to American Legation, Cairo;
One Copy to American Legation, Baghdad.

This agreement made between His Excellency, Shaikh Abdulla Suleiman Al Hamdan, Minister of Finance of Saudi Arabia, acting on behalf of the Saudi Arab Government (hereinafter referred to as the "Government") of the one part, and L. N. Hamilton, acting on behalf of Standard Oil Company of California (hereinafter referred to as the "Company") of the other part.

It is hereby agreed between the Government and the Company in manner following:

Article 1: The Government hereby grants to the Company on the terms and conditions hereinafter mentioned, and with respect to the area defined below, the exclusive right, for a period of sixty years from the effective date hereof, to explore, prospect, drill for, extract, treat, manufacture, transport, deal with, carry away and export petroleum, asphalt, naptha, natural greases, ozokerite, and other hydrocarbons, and the derivatives of all such products. It is understood, however, that such right does not include the exclusive right to sell crude or refined products within the area described below or within Saudi Arabia.

Article 2: The area covered by the exclusive right referred to in Article 1 hereof is all of eastern Saudi Arabia, from its eastern boundary (including islands and territorial waters) westward to the westerly edge of the Dahana, and from the northern boundary to the southern boundary of Saudi Arabia, provided that from the northern end of the westerly edge of the Dahana the westerly boundary of the area in question shall continue in a straight line north thirty degrees west to the northern boundary of Saudi Arabia, and from the southern end of the westerly edge of the Dahana such boundary shall continue in a straight line south thirty degrees east to the southern boundary of Saudi Arabia.

For convenience this area may be referred to as the "exclusive Area".

Article 3: In addition to the grant of the exclusive area described in Article 2 of this agreement, the Government also hereby grants to the Company a preference right to acquire an oil concession covering the balance of eastern Saudi Arabia extending as far west of the westerly boundary of the exclusive area as the contact between the sedimentary and igneous formations. This preference right includes such rights as the Government may now have, or may hereafter acquire, in the so-called Neutral Zone bordering on the Persian Gulf to the south of Kuwait. The nature of this preference right is to be hereafter agreed upon. The term "oil concession" as used in this Article means an exclusive concession covering the same products which are covered by the present agreement.

Furthermore, the Company's geologists shall have the right to examine the region covered by the preference right just referred to (excepting the neutral zone referred to above), in so far as such examination may be necessary or advisable for a better understanding of the geological character of the exclusive area.

Article 4: Within the time agreed in Article 18 of this agreement, the Company shall make an initial loan to the Government of thirty thousand pounds, gold, or its equivalent.

Article 5: The Company shall pay the Government annually the sum of five thousand pounds, gold, or its equivalent. For convenience this payment is termed an annual rental and it is payable in advance. The first annual rental shall be paid within the time agreed in Article 18 of this agreement; thereafter, so long as the contract is not terminated, the annual rental shall be due upon each anniversary of the effective date hereof and shall be payable within thirty days after such anniversary, provided that upon the commercial discovery of oil no further annual rentals shall be due or payable.

Article 6: If this contract has not been terminated within eighteen months from the effective date hereof, the Company shall make a second loan to the Government, amounting to twenty thousand pounds, gold, or its equivalent. The due date of such loan shall be eighteen months from the effective date hereof but the Company shall have fifteen days from the due date within which to make the loan.

Article 7: During the life of this agreement, the Government shall be under no obligation to repay the initial loan of £ 30,000, gold, (or its equivalent), or the second loan of £ 20,000, gold, (or its equivalent). The Company shall have the right to recover the amount of these two loans by way of deductions from one-half of the royalties due the Government. If the amount of the two loans, in whole or in part, shall not have been so recovered by the Company upon the termination of this contract, the Government shall repay the unrecovered amount in four equal and consecutive annual instalments, the first instalment to be paid within one year from the date of the termination of this agreement. Furthermore until such unrecovered amount has been repaid by the Government, the Company's preference right, referred to in Article 3 hereof, shall continue in force.

Article 8: Upon the effective date of this agreement, the Company shall commence plans and preparations for geological work, so planning the work as to take advantage of the cooler season for more efficient work in the field.

and of the hotter season for the necessary office work of compiling data and reports. In any event, the actual field work shall commence not later than the end of September, 1933, and it shall be continued diligently until operations connected with drilling are commenced, or until the contract is terminated.

Article 9: Within ninety days after the commencement of drilling, the Company shall relinquish to the Government such portions of the exclusive area as the Company at that time may decide not to explore further, or to use otherwise in connection with this enterprise. Similarly, from time to time during the life of this contract, the Company shall relinquish to the Government such further portions of the exclusive area as the Company may then decide not to explore or prospect further, or to use otherwise in connection with the enterprise. The portions so relinquished shall thereupon be released from the terms and conditions of this contract, excepting only that during the life of this contract the Company shall continue to enjoy the right to use the portions so relinquished for transportation and communication facilities, which however shall interfere as little as practicable with any other use to which the relinquished portions may be put.

Article 10: The Company shall commence operations connected with drilling as soon as a suitable structure has been found, and in any event if the Company does not commence such operations within three years from the end of September, 1933 (subject to the provisions of Article 27 hereof), the Government may terminate this contract. Once commenced, these operations shall be continued diligently until oil in commercial quantities has been discovered, or until this agreement is terminated. If the Company should fail to declare so sooner, the date of discovery of oil in commercial quantities shall be the date upon which the Company has completed and tested a well or wells capable of producing, in accordance with first-class oilfield practice, at least two thousand tons of oil per day for a period of thirty consecutive days.

Operations connected with drilling include the ordering and shipping of materials and equipment to Saudi Arabia, the construction of roads, camps, buildings, structures, communication facilities, etc., and the installation and operation of the machinery, equipment and facilities for drilling wells.

Article 11: Upon the discovery of oil in commercial quantities, the Company shall advance to the Government the sum of fifty thousand pounds, gold, or its equivalent, and one year later the further sum of fifty thousand pounds, gold, or its equivalent. The due date of the first advance shall be the date of discovery of oil in commercial quantities, as provided in Article 10 hereof, and the due date of the second advance shall be one year

-4-

later. In each case the Company shall have sixty days following the due date within which to make the advance. Both of these advances are on account of royalties which may be due the Government and consequently the Company shall have the right to recover the amount of these advances by way of deductions from one-half of the royalties due the Government.

Article 12: Since it has been agreed that the annual rental of five thousand pounds, gold, or its equivalent, is payable to the date of the discovery of oil in commercial quantities, and since it has been agreed also that this annual rental is to be payable in advance, it may happen that the last annual rental paid prior to the date of discovery of oil in commercial quantities will cover a period beyond the date of such discovery. In case that this period should be equal to or greater than one-fifth of a year, the proportionate amount of the five thousand pounds, gold, or its equivalent, corresponding to such period shall be treated as an advance on account of royalties due the Government, and consequently it shall be recoverable by the Company by way of deductions from one-half of the royalties due the Government.

Article 13: As soon as practicable (i.e., allowing a reasonable time for ordering and shipping further materials and equipment to Saudi Arabia and commencing further work) after the date of discovering of oil in commercial quantities, the Company shall continue operations connected with drilling by using at least two strings of tools. These operations shall be continued diligently until the proven area has been drilled up in accordance with first-class oilfield practice, or until the contract is terminated.

Article 14: The Company shall pay the Government a royalty on all net crude oil produced and saved and run from field storage, after first deducting:

(1) water and foreign substances; and

(2) oil required for the customary operations of the Company's installations within Saudi Arabia; and

(3) the oil required for manufacturing the amounts of gasoline and kerosene to be provided free each year to the Government in accordance with Article 19 hereof.

The rate of royalty per ton of such net crude oil shall be either:

(a) four shillings, gold, or its equivalent; or

(b) at the election of the Company at the time of making each royalty payment, one dollar, United States currency, plus the amount, if

any, by which the average rate of
exchange of four shillings, gold, during
the last half of the semester for which
the royalty payment is due, may exceed one
dollar and ten cents, United States
currency. Thus, for example, if such
average rate should be one dollar and
fourteen cents, United States currency
(that is to say, five dollars and seventy
cents per gold pound), the royalty rate
would be one dollar and four cents,
United States currency, per ton of such
net crude oil.

Article 15: If the Company should produce, save and
sell any natural gas, it will pay to the Government a
royalty equal to one-eighth of the proceeds of the sale of
such natural gas, it being understood however that the
Company shall be under no obligation to produce, save, sell,
or otherwise dispose of any natural gas. It is also understood that the Company is under no obligation to pay any
royalty on such natural gas as it may use for the customary
operations of its installations within Saudi Arabia.

Article 16: The Government, through duly authorized
representatives, may, during the usual hours of operations,
inspect and examine the operations of the Company under
this contract and may verify the amount of production.
The Company shall measure in accordance with first-class
oilfield practice the amount of oil produced and saved
and run from field storage, and shall keep true and
correct accounts thereof, and of any natural gas it may
produce and save and sell, and duly authorized representatives
of the Government shall also have access at all reasonable
times to such accounts. The Company shall, within three
months after the end of each semester, commencing with
the date of commercial discovery of oil, deliver to the
Government an abstract of such accounts for the semester,
and a statement of the amount of royalties due the Government for the semester. These accounts and statements shall
be treated as confidential by the Government, with the
exception of such items therein as the Government may be
required to publish for fiscal purposes.

The royalties due the Government at the end of each
semester, commencing with the date of commercial discovery
of oil, shall be paid within three months after the end of
the semester. In case of any question as to the amount of
royalties due for any semester, such portion of the amount
as may be unquestioned shall be tendered the Government
within the period hereinabove provided, and thereupon
the question shall be settled by agreement between the
parties, or failing that, by arbitration as provided in
this contract. Any further sum which may be payable to
the Government as a result of this settlement shall be paid
within sixty days after the date of such settlement.

<u>Article 17</u>: It is agreed that all gold payments provided in this contract, whether pounds gold or shillings gold, are to be based on the gold pound standard according to its weight and fineness at the time the payments may be due. It is also agreed that wherever it is stipulated in this contract that the equivalent of any sum or amount in pounds gold or in shillings gold may be paid, such equivalent may be dollars in United States currency, or pounds sterling.

It is agreed furthermore that the equivalent of pounds gold or shillings gold, for any payment which may be made hereunder in dollars, United States currency, or in pounds sterling (with the exception of the first payment provided for in Article 18 hereof) shall be based on the average of the rate of exchange as computed over a period of three months immediately preceding the due date of the payment.

<u>Article 18</u>: All payments provided in this contract to be made to the Government may be made by tendering such payments directly to the Government, or by depositing the amount due to the credit of the Government in some bank which the Government designates in writing and which the Government may change from time to time by giving written notice to the Company long enough in advance so that the Company will have sufficient time to make future payments to the new bank. It is agreed that the Government will designate such bank in Saudi Arabia, or in the United States of America, or in England, or in Holland, but that no bank in Saudi Arabia will be so designated unless such bank has a correspondent in United States of America, England or Holland through which bank transfers of money to Saudi Arabia may be made. Once the Company has made the proper payment to the Government, or has deposited the proper sum in any such bank, or has paid the sum to such correspondent for transfer to a bank in Saudi Arabia, the Company shall be free of all further responsibility in connection with the payment.

It is agreed, however, that the first payment of thirty-five thousand pounds, gold, or its equivalent, (comprising the initial loan and the first annual rental) shall be made, within fifteen days after the effective date of this agreement, to a correspondent, in New York or in London, of Netherlands Trading Society (Nederlandsche Handel-Maatschappij) at Jeddah, Saudi Arabia, to be transmitted without delay, and at the expense of the Company, to said Society and to be delivered to the Government upon obtaining a proper receipt from the Government for such payment. If this first payment is not made in gold, it will be made in pounds sterling at the current rate of exchange at the time the Company makes the payment to such correspondent.

<u>Article 19</u>: As soon as practicable after the date of discovery of oil in commercial quantities, the Company shall select somepoint within Saudi Arabia for the erection of a plant for manufacturing sufficient gasoline

and kerosene to meet the ordinary requirements of the Government, providing of course that the character of the crude oil found will permit of the manufacture of such products on a commercial basis by the use of ordinary refining methods, and provided further that the amount of oil developed is sufficient for the purpose. It is understood that the ordinary requirements of the Government shall not include resale inside or outside of the country. Upon the completion of the necessary preliminary arrangements, and as soon as the Company has obtained the Government's consent to the proposed location, the Company shall proceed with the erection of such plant. During each year following the date of completion of this plant, the Company shall offer free to the Government, in bulk, two hundred thousand American gallons of gasoline and one hundred thousand American gallons of kerosene, it being understood that the facilities provided by the Government for accepting these deliveries shall not impede or endanger the Company's operations.

Article 20: The Company, at its own expense, will employ the necessary number of guards and guides to protect its representatives, its camps and installations. The Government promises to cooperate fully in supplying the best soldiers and men available for this responsibility, and in furnishing every reasonable protection, at rates not exceeding those customarily paid by the Government or others for similar services, it being understood that the expense for such services shall be paid by the Company through the Government.

Article 21: In return for the obligations assumed by the Company under this contract, and for the payments required from the Company hereunder, the Company and enterprise shall be exempt from all direct and indirect taxes, imposts, charges, fees and duties (including, of course, import and export duties), it being understood that this privilege shall not extend to the sale of products within the country, nor shall it extend to the personal requirements of the individual employees of the Company. Any materials imported free of duty may not be sold within the country without first paying the corresponding import duty.

Article 22: It is understood, of course, that the Company has the right to use all means and facilities it may deem necessary or advisable in order to exercise the rights granted under this contract, so as to carry out the purposes of this enterprise, including, among other things, the right to construct and use roads, camps, buildings, structures and all systems of communication; to instal and operate machinery, equipment and facilities in connection with the drilling of wells, or in connection with the transportation, storage, treatment, manufacture, dealing with, or exportation of petroleum or its derivatives, or in connection with the camps, building and quarters of the personnel of the Company; to construct and use storage reservoirs, tanks and receptacles; to construct and operate wharves, piers, sea-loading lines and all other terminal and port facilities; and to use all forms of transportation of personnel or equipment, and of petroleum and its derivatives. It is understood, however, that the use of aeroplanes within the country shall be the subject of a separate agreement.

The Company shall also have the right to develop, carry away and use water. It likewise shall have the right to carry away and use any water belonging to the Government, for the operations of the enterprise, but so as not to prejudice irrigation or to deprive any lands, houses, or watering places for cattle, of a reasonable supply of water from time to time.

The Company may also take and use, but only to the extent necessary for the purposes of the enterprise, other natural products belonging to the Government, such as surface soil, timber, stone, lime, gypsum, stone and similar substances.

Government officials and agents, in pursuance of official business, shall have the right to use such communication and transportation facilities as the Company may establish, provided that such use shall not obstruct or interfere with the Company's operations hereunder and shall not impose upon the Company any substantial burden of expense.

In times of national emergency, the use of the Company's transportation and communication facilities by the Government shall entitle the Company to fair compensation for any loss it may sustain thereby, whether through damages to the Company's facilities, equipment or installations or through the obstruction or interference with the Company's operations.

Article 23: The enterprise under this contract shall be directed and supervised by Americans who shall employ Saudi Arab nationals as far as practicable, and in so far as the Company can find suitable Saudi Arab employees it will not employ other nationals.

In respect of the treatment of workers, the Company shall abide by the existing laws of the country applicable generally to workers of any other industrial enterprise.

Article 24: The Government reserves the right to search for and obtain any substances or products, other than those exclusively granted by this contract, within the area covered by this agreement, except lands occupied by wells or other installations of the Company, provided always that the right thus reserved by the Government shall be exercised so as not to endanger the operations of the Company or interfere with its rights hereunder, and provided also that a fair compensation shall be paid the

-9-

Company by the Government for all damage the Company may
sustain through the exercise of the right so reserved by
the Government. In any grant of such right so reserved by
the Government, the concessionaire shall be bound by the
provisions of this Article.

Article 25: The Company is hereby empowered by the
Government to acquire from any occupant the surface rights
of any land which the Company may find necessary to use in
connection with the enterprise, provided that the Company
shall pay the occupant for depriving him of the use of the
land. The payment shall be a fair one with respect to the
customary use made of the land by the occupant. The Government will lend every reasonable assistance to the Company
in case of any difficulties with respect to acquiring the
rights of a surface occupant.

The Company, of course, shall have no right to acquire
or to occupy Holy Places.

Article 26: The Company shall supply the Government
with copies of all topographical maps and geological
reports (as finally made and approved by the Company)
relating to the exploration and exploitation of the area
covered by this contract. The Company shall also furnish
the Government, within four months after the end of each
year, commencing with the date of commercial discovery
of oil, a report of the operations under this contract
during the year. These maps and reports shall be treated
as confidential by the Government.

Article 27: No failure or omission on the part of
the Company to carry out or to perform any of the terms
or conditions of this contract shall give the Government
any claim against the Company, or be deemed a breach of
this contract, in so far as such failure or omission may
arise from force majeure. If through force majeure the
fulfillment of any term or condition of this contract
should be delayed, the period of the delay, together
with such period as may be required for the restoration of
any damage done during such delay, shall be added to the
terms or periods fixed in this contract.

Article 28: The Company may terminate this contract
at any time by giving the Government thirty days' advance
notice in writing, whether by letter or by telegraph,
provided that the telegraphic notice is promptly confirmed
by letter. Upon the termination of this contract through
such notice, or through any other cause, the Government
and the Company shall thereafter be free of all further
obligations under this contract except as follows:

1. The Company's immovable property, such as roads,
water or oil wells with their casings, permanent buildings
and structures, etc., shall become the property of the
Government free of charge.

2. The Company shall afford the Government an opportunity to purchase the movable property of the enterprise in Saudi Arabia at a fair price equal to the replacement value of such property at the time less depreciation. Any controversy about this fair price shall be settled by arbitration in the same manner as provided in Article 31 of this contract. If the Government declines or fails, within two months following the date of the termination of this contract, to purchase such movable property, or if the Government fails to tender the purchase price within thirty days after it has been decided upon, by agreement or by arbitration, the Company shall then have six months within which to remove such property.

3. If, in accordance with Article 7 of this contract, there is any unrecovered amount still due the Company, the provisions of Article 7 shall remain in force until the obligation therein mentioned has been satisfied.

Article 29: In case of the breach by the Company of its obligation to make the second loan of twenty thousand pounds, gold, or its equivalent, as provided in Article 6 hereof, or of its obligation to commence operations connected with drilling as set forth in Article 10 hereof, or of its obligation to make the two advances each of fifty thousand pounds, gold, or the equivalent, under the terms and conditions provided in Article 11 hereof, or of its obligation under Article 30 hereof to pay the amount of any damages which may be assessed upon the Company, the Government's remedy shall be the right to give the Company notice at once of such breach, and thereupon if the Company does not take immediate steps to comply with the obligation so breached, the Government may terminate this contract.

Article 30: Except as otherwise provided in Article 29 hereof, the penalty for the breach by the Company of any of its obligations under this contract shall be damages which shall be payable to the Government under the following conditions:

The Government shall at once notify the Company of any alleged breach on the part of the Company, setting forth the nature of such breach. Any controversy which may arise as to whether or not the Company has committed the alleged breach shall be settled by arbitration in the manner provided in this agreement. Once that the fact of the commission of the breach has been established, the failure of the Company to take immediate steps to remedy the breach shall subject the Company to the payment of damages to the Government, and if such damages cannot be agreed upon they shall be determined by arbitration in the manner provided in this contract. The amount of any damages which may be so determined shall be paid to the Government by the Company within sixty days after such determination.

Article 31: If any doubt, difference, or dispute shall arise between the Government and the Company concerning the interpretation or execution of this contract, or anything herein contained or in connection herewith, or the rights and liabilities of the parties hereunder, it shall, failing any agreement to settle it in another way, be referred to two arbitrators, one of whom shall be chosen by each party, and a referee who shall be chosen by the Arbitrators before proceeding to arbitration. Such party shall nominate its arbitrator within thirty days of being requested in writing by the other party to do so. In the event of the arbitrators failing to agree upon a referee, the Government and the Company shall, in agreement, appoint a referee, and in the event of their failing to agree they shall request the President of the Permanent Court of International Justice to appoint a referee. The decision of the arbitrators, or in the case of a difference of opinion between them, the decision of the referee, shall be final. The place of arbitration shall be such as may be agreed upon by the Parties, and in default of agreement, shall be The Hague, Holland.

Article 32: The Company may not, without the consent of the Government, assign its rights and obligations under this contract to anyone, but it is understood that the Company, upon notifying the Government, shall have the right to assign its rights and obligations hereunder to a corporation it may organize exclusively for the purposes of this enterprise. The Company shall also have the right to create such other corporations and organizations as it may consider necessary or advisable for the purposes of this enterprise. Any such corporation or organization, upon being invested with any or all of the rights and obligations under this contract, and upon notification thereof to the Government, shall thereupon be subject to the terms and conditions of this agreement.

In the event that the shares of stock issued by any such corporation or organization should be offered for sale to the general public, the inhabitants of Saudi Arabia shall be allowed a reasonable time to subscribe (upon similar terms and conditions offered to others) for at least twenty per cent of such shares of stock so issued and offered for sale to the general public.

Article 33: It is understood that the periods of time referred to in this agreement shall be reckoned on the basis of the solar calendar.

Article 34: The effective date of this contract shall be the date of its publication in Saudi Arabia, following the ratification of this contract by the Company.

Article 35: This contract has been drawn up in English and in Arabic. Inasmuch as most of the obligations hereunder are imposed upon the Company and inasmuch as the interpretation of the English text, especially as regards techmical obligations and requirements relating to the oil industry, has been fairly well established through long practice and experience in contracts such as the present one, it is agreed that while both texts shall have equal validity, nevertheless in case of any divergence of interpretation as to the Company's obligations hereunder, the English text shall prevail.

Article 36: To avoid any doubt on the point, it is distinctly understood that the Company or anyone connected with it shall have no right to interfere with the administrative, political or religious affairs within Saudi Arabia.

Article 37: It is understood that this contract, after being signed in Saudi Arabia, shall be subject to ratification by the Company at its offices in San Francisco, California, before it shall become effective. After both texts of this contract have been signed in duplicate in Saudi Arabia, the signed copies shall be sent by registered mail in the next outgoing mail to the Company in San Francisco, California, and within fifteen days after receipt in San Francisco, the Company shall transmit to the Government by telegraph whether or not it ratifies this contract. If the contract is not ratified by the Company within fifteen days after receipt of the document in San Francisco, it shall be null and void and of no further force or effect.

Likewise, if the amount of the initial loan and the first annual rental is not paid within the time agreed upon in Article 18 hereof, the Government may declare this contract to be null and void and of no further force or effect.

Upon ratification of this contract by the Company, one signed copy of each text, together with the necessary evidence as to ratification by the Company, shall be returned to the Government. Also upon ratification of this contract by the Company, the contract shall be published in Saudi Arabia in the usual manner.

Signed this 29th day of May, 1933 (corresponding to the 4th day of Safar, 1352, A.H.).

On behalf of Saudi Arab Government

On behalf of Standard Oil
Company of California

Jedda, Saudi Arabia.
May 29, 1933.
(corresponding to the 4th
of Safar, 1932, A.H.)

His Excellency
Shaikh Abdulla Suleiman Al Hamdan,
Jedda, Saudi Arabia.

Dear Shaikh Abdulla:

Referring to the contract which has been signed today
by you, on behalf of the Saudi Arab Government, and by the
undersigned, on behalf of Standard Oil Company of California,
relative to an oil concession covering a portion of eastern
Saudi Arabia, I am setting forth below the agreement we
have also reached on behalf of the two parties to the same
contract, which agreement shall be considered as a part of
the said contract. For convenience, the two parties in
question shall be referred to below in the same manner as
designated in the said contract, namely, the "Government"
and the "Company", and the said contract shall be referred
to as the "Saudi Arab Concession".

1. The Company is granted a preference right to an
oil concession covering a certain area described in Article
3 of the Saudi Arab Concession. The preference right so
granted the Company shall be a right to acquire an oil
concession covering such area, exclusive of the so-called
Neutral Zone also referred to in the same Article 3, by
equalling the terms of any offer for such concession that
may be made the Government by others in good faith and
that the Government may be ready and willing to accept.
Within thirty days after receiving from the Government
written notice, setting forth in full the terms of such
offer, the Company shall notify the Government whether or
not the Company wishes to acquire the oil concession by
equalling the terms so offered. If the Company does not
wish to do so, the Government is free to accept the offer
made, but if an oil concession should not be granted to
others on the same terms as those so offered and so presented
to the Company, the preference right of the Company shall
continue, at least so long as the provisions of Article 7
of the Sandi Arab Concession remain in force.

2. The Company's preference right to acquire an oil
concession covering the so-called Neutral Zone referred to
in Article 3 of the Saudi Arab Concession, shall be a right
to equal, with respect to the rights of the Government in
the Neutral Zone, the terms and conditions which may be
obtained by the Shaikh of Kuwait for a concession covering
his rights in the Neutral Zone. In the absence of any grant
of an oil concession covering such rights of the Shaikh of

-2-

Kuwait, the Government will endeavor to reach an agreement
with the Shaikh Kuwait whereby the Company will be permitted
to acquire an oil concession covering the rights of the
Government and of the Shaikh of Kuwait in the Neutral Zone.
In either of these two events, the Company shall have a
period of thirty days from the date it receives written
notice setting forth in full the terms and conditions of
the oil concession covering the rights of the Shaikh of
Kuwait in the Neutral Zone, or covering the terms of the
proposed concession embracing the rights of the Government
and of the Shaikh of Kuwait in the Neutral Zone, as the
case may be, within which to decide and to notify the Government whether or not the Company wishes to acquire the oil
concession on such terms. If the Company does not wish to
do so, the Government is free to negotiate with others,
but if the oil concession should not be granted to others
on the same terms as those offered to the Company, the
preference right of the Company shall continue, at least
so long as the provisions of Article 7 of the Saudi Arab
Concession remain in force.

3. Article 22 of the Saudi Arab Concession states
that the use of aeroplanes shall be the subject of a
separate agreement. One purpose of the present letter is
to set forth the agreement as to this point. In view of
the restrictions now prevailing in Saudi Arabia as to the
use of aeroplanes within the country by anyone other than
the Government, it is hereby agreed that so long as such
restrictions remain in force, the Government will undertake to provide, at the request and at the expense of the
Company, such aeroplane service as the Company may consider
advisable for the purpose of its operations within the
area covered by the Saudi Arab Concession. Such service
shall be limited to the purposes of the enterprise. If
any aeroplane photographs should be taken for geological
or mapping purposes, the Government and the Company shall
each receive copies, also at the expense of the Company.

4. The consent of the Government must be obtained
before the Company shall have any right to examine the
so-called Neutral Zone referred to in Article 3 of the
Saudi Arab Concession.

5. The provisions of Article 35 of the Saudi Arab
Concession shall also apply to this agreement.

- - - - - -

In order to confirm the above agreement, will you
be kind enough to sign below under the heading "Agreement
Confirmed". I am sending this letter in triplicate,
and upon the return of two copies signed by you, as well
as the two signed copies of the Arabic text, they will be
forwarded with the Saudi Arab Concession to the offices
of the Company in San Francisco for ratification by the

-5-

Company there, after which one signed and ratified
copy of the English and Arabic text hereof will be
returned to the Government.

Very truly yours,

On behalf of Standard Oil
Company of California.

Agreement Confirmed:

On behalf of the Saudi
Arab Government.

NO. 19.

AMERICAN CONSULATE,

Aden, Arabia, June 24, 1933.

CONFIDENTIAL

SUBJECT: Oil Concession for the Al Hassa Area of Saudi
Arabia.

THE HONORABLE

THE SECRETARY OF STATE,

WASHINGTON.

I have the honor to inform the Department that the following notice appeared in the June 2nd issued of UM EL QURA:

"An agreement has been signed by both the Minister of
Finance and a representative of the Standerd Oil
Company of California by which a concession has been
given to the latter to exploit the fuel oil and its
similar products for the eastern provinces of the
Kingdom mentioned in the text of the agreement.
The publication of the agreement will take place
after the sanction of the Government and the Executive Committee of the said company, very soon."

It has been learned from a representative of the Socony-
Vacuum Corporation, for the Red Sea area, that there were
three contestants for this concession, namely:

The Standard Oil Company of California,
The Iraq Petroleum Company, and, a
Major Holmes, British, Concession Broker.

The Major Holmes mentioned is a British subject who is
very conversant with conditions in this part of the East; he
is rated as an adventurer in finance and operates as a concession broker, sometimes on his own and at other times for
the Eastern General Syndicate which, in itself, is rated as
a concession brokerage concern. In this present instance it
is not known whether Homles was operating individually or as
a representative of the above-mentioned syndicate. However,
he remained only two days at Djedda on this oil deal; it is

890F.6363 STANDARD OIL CO./17

AUG 4 - 1933

-2-

thought he realized the seriousness of the California Company's tender and, having no inside track with the Saudian government, pulled out for more probable undertakings elsewhere.

The Iraq Petroleum Company was represented by a certain Mr. Longrigg, a British national. It is not believed the representative was seriously interested in the objective set for him, since it is reported that he was mostly away on a hunting or fishing trip and had scarsely any contact with the government representatives upon their visits to Djedda to talk over these matters.

The negotiations on the part of the Standard Oil Co. of California were entrusted to a certain Mr. Hamilton, who came from the United States for that purpose; he was assisted by Mr. K. S. Twitchell who accompanied him. It will be re-called that Mr. Twitchell was formerly acting for Mr. Charles R. Crane in building the bridge on the road between Hodeidah and San'aa in the Yemen; he also made a rather general mineral survey of Hedjaz-Nejd area. Just what his actual connection with the present negotiations was, is not known; perhaps his previous acquaintance with Saudi Arabian affairs and officials was thought to be of value, or a further agreement looking toward wider oil and mineral prospecting is in contemplation.

For the present at least, the concession contemplates the exploitation of the mainland adjacent to the Island of Bahrein in the Persian Gulf area; the Standard Oil Co. of California is already operating on this Island and it is the purpose of this concession to permit the company to extend its operations to the mainland, in the vicinity thereof.

The terms of the Saudian Government were first said to have been the down payment by the company of between 100,000 and 200,000 pounds Sterling for the concession rights; the

94

interest on this amount was to serve as the prospecting fees, and the principal was to be retired by credit against certain undetermined royalties to be paid by the company on the oils to be produced. Native labor was to be employed as much as possible, and the entire plant, materials, rolling stock, et cetera were to become the property of the government at the expiration of the concession.

The down payment of such a large sum on a win-or-loose basis was not appealing; the final clause also did not prove an inducement. It was the desire of the company to make a fixed down payment upon the striking of oil in quantity, and the payment thereafter of fixed semi-annual sums.

Just what are the final terms of the concession are not known at present.

Respectfully yours,

Ray Fox
American Consul

File No. 863.6.
RF/msm

June 26 1933

Dear Mr. Twitchell:

Many thanks for your letter of June 1 telling me
of the success of your mission in obtaining a concession
for the exploration and development of petroleum resources in Eastern Saudi Arabia. We received similar
information from Mr. Loomis a couple of weeks ago and
he has agreed to let us have a copy of the concession
as soon as he receives the original.

Considering the slowness with which matters usually
move in the East I think that you and Mr. Hamilton are
to be congratulated upon the dispatch with which you
arrived at an agreement with the Arabian Government.
It is to be hoped that the entrance of foreign capital
into Saudi Arabia will be helpful in developing the
prosperity of that country, and I have no doubt that
it will lead to closer relations between Ibn Saud's
Government and our own. Under present conditions I
imagine that the Department would find it difficult
to give immediate consideration to the question of

Mr. K. S. Twitchell,
    Jedda,
        Hedjaz,
            Saudi Arabia.

- 2 -

official representation at Jedda, but if relations between the two countries develop as we hope they will the question of representation will certainly have to be considered within the next two or three years.

For your own information I might add that we have not yet concluded the proposed exchange of notes with the Arabian Government, but the matter is progressing and I am hopeful that the agreement will be signed within the next month or two.

With best wishes, I am,

Yours very sincerely,

Wallace Murray,
Chief, Division of Near Eastern Affairs.

NE PHA/LS

K.S.TWITCHELL
MINING ENGINEER
555 FIFTH AVENUE
NEW YORK CITY

Jedda August 10 1933
Hijaz,
Saudi Arabia.

acd. 8/9/33
HSr/LS

July 15,1933.

Wallace Murray,Esq.,
Chief of Div. of the Near East,
Department of State,
Washington,D.C.

Dear Mr.Murray;

Although I wrote you on June 1, I am going to inflict another letter upon you as I think you may be intrested in knowing that the oil concession in which I am interested was ratified by the Board of D1ectors of the Standrd Oil Co. of Calif. at San Francisco on July 5 . It was ratified by King Ibn Saud on July 7, and published in a special edition of the Governm ent newspaper at Mecca on July 16th.

The Company has asked me to attend to the formalitis of the ratification and publishing here and to the making of the first payment of rental andloan. The articles of the Concessi ie. the first sixteen, were published in the official newspaper yesterday. The others will be printed in succeeding issues. The Government is not publishing details of the loans and payments, as it wishes to avoid the critism of those who might say it should have obtained terms equal to the Iraq and Persian governments. This Government understands that the conditions here are quite different from those of the other two countries. I consider our concession to be extremely fair, even generous, and - if commercial oil is found it will add enormously to the prosperity of this country.

How is the U.S.A treaty progressing ? What are the possibilities of a U.S.Legation or Consulate here? Pardon my questio

Yours sincerely,
K.S.Twitchell

DEPARTMENT OF STATE

NEAR EAST...

DIVISION OF NEAR EASTERN AFFAIRS   July 11 1933

July 17, 1933.

Francis B. Loomis, of the Standard Oil Company of California, called on me this morning to make certain inquiries in connection with the oil concession for El Hasa recently obtained by his Company from Ibn Saud, King of Saudi Arabia.

Mr. Loomis left me the attached map of Arabia. His Company is particularly concerned over the western boundary of the British Hinterland of Aden, particularly that portion thereof west of El Qatar and Trucial Oman. He says that his Company's geologists think there is oil in the territory between El Qatar, Trucial Oman and the boundary line of the British Hinterland of Aden, which territory is marked in red on the attached map. Mr. Loomis says that his Company's geologists desire to start their explorations at this particular point and wonder whether they are likely to get into any trouble with the British or the Sheikh of El Qatar.

Mr. Loomis asked me whether we had any information on the subject of this boundary line in addition to that contained in the Statesman's Year Book for 1930. I told Mr. Loomis that we would look into the matter and be glad to let him have any information available to the Department.

WSM/GC

MANDATES IN ARABIA

FIGURE 16

Compiled by
Col. Lawrence Martin

[23]

From "International Conciliation, May, 1924. No. 198.
Apparently based on Anglo-Turkish Convention of 1914
as to "British Hinterland of Aden."

DEPARTMENT OF STATE

———

DIVISION OF NEAR EASTERN AFFAIRS

46° 5' 0"

15° 00' N , 46° 4' 0" E of Greenwich

NE 本

20° 00' N., 50° 21' 30" E

July 21 1955

My dear Mr. Loomis:

I have looked into the question of the western boundary of the British Hinterland of Aden which you brought up in our recent conversation.

We have no definite or conclusive information on the subject but the data which we have found may be of some assistance to you. Apparently that section of the western boundary in which you are interested was defined by the Anglo-Turkish Convention of 1913. We have copies of three articles of that Convention but according to a statement of the British Resident on the Persian Gulf the remainder of the Convention is confidential. The same official refers to the Convention as the "unratified Anglo-Turkish Agreement of 1913". I should add that those articles of the Convention which have been furnished to

The Honorable
    Francis B. Loomis,
        225 Bush Street,
            San Francisco, California.

-2-

us are not pertinent to the boundary in which you are
interested.

Although we are without definite information it is
our belief that the boundary in question is probably
correctly set forth in a map which was submitted by the
British Foreign Office to the Turkish Petroleum Company
through the British group interested in that Company
several years ago. On that map the western boundary of
the Hinterland, after leaving the Aden Protectorate, proceeds from approximately 15° 0' 0" north, 46° 4' 0" east
of Greenwich in a straight line in a northeasterly direction to about 20° 0' 0" north, 50° 21' 30" east. From
that point it runs due north to the Persian Gulf in a line
which if extended would appear to skirt the western edge
of the Island of Bahrein. The degrees of latitude and
longitude which I have mentioned above are perhaps not
strictly accurate since the map from which we took them
is of small scale and it is impossible to make from it an
accurate calculation. Assuming, however, that this boundary
is approximately correct, it would appear to be somewhat
more favorable to your interests than the western boundary
as delineated on the map appearing in International Conciliation, May, 1924, a copy of which you left with me.

I hope that this information will be of assistance to
you and in the event that we find anything more definite

—+—

with respect to the boundary, I shall be glad to pass
it on to you.

Sincerely yours,

Wallace Murray
Chief, Division of Near Eastern Affairs.

NE PHA/LVD   HA
                              SWB

JUL 21, 1938

NO. 174

382

AMERICAN CONSULATE
Cairo, Egypt, August 1, 1933.

890F.6363 IRAQ PETROLEUM CO./1

IRAQ PETROLEUM COMPANY NEGOTIATIONS FOR OIL CONCESSION IN ASSIR.

FOR DISTRIBUTION - CHECK   Yes   No
To the Field
U. S. A.

THE HONORABLE

THE SECRETARY OF STATE

WASHINGTON

SIR:

I have the honor to report that the issue of August 1, 1933, of the Egyptian Gazette, an English daily paper published in Egypt, contained the following news item indicating that the Iraq Petroleum Company is negotiating with the Government of Saudia Arabia for an oil concession in Assir.

"OIL PRODUCTION IN ASSIR.

"Al Ahram's Jerusalem correspondent states that he learns from a very reliable source that the Iraq Petroleum Company has begun negotiations with the Government of the Arab Saudi Kingdom on the subject of obtaining a concession for prospecting for oil in Assir."

Although this office has no confirmation of the above-mentioned report, it is believed to be very probable that the Iraq Petroleum Company has become interested in the prospect of discovering petroleum resources in Assir, inasmuch as the Company previously endeavored to secure an oil concession embracing the

- 2 -

area included in the Concession recently granted to
the Standard Oil Company of California.

Respectfully yours,

Gordon P. Merriam,
American Consul.

File No. 863.6
RYB/am.

CABLE ADDRESS
NATGEOSOC,WASHINGTON

National Geographic Society

WASHINGTON, D. C.

GILBERT GROSVENOR, PRESIDENT
JOHN JOY EDSON, TREASURER

JOHN OLIVER LA GORCE, VICE PRESIDENT
GEORGE W. HUTCHISON, SECRETARY,

February 20, 1934.

Mr. K. S. Twitchell,
522 Fifth Avenue,
New York City.

Dear Mr. Twitchell:

Your letter of January 22 to Mr. Simpich has been referred to me because of your comments on our Asia map which was drawn in my department.

I, too, wish that you could have seen this map before it was published so that it could have had the benefit of your first-hand knowledge of Arabia which seems to be the most difficult region to show correctly on a map.

We had the help of the State Department and the Statesman's Year Book and hoped that we were showing as well as possible the loose and changing political relationship of the various parts.

According to our State Department and the Statesman's Year Book, Hadhramaut is loosely under British protection and control. Also we have not shown the "British Hinterland of Aden" in the same status as the "Aden Protectorate." A study of our type styles and of the explanation of types in the upper right-hand corner will clear this up.

About the Rub-al-Khali: Our boundary of Saudi-Arabia was furnished to us by the State Department after its recognition of that country. The use of this boundary also causes the objection regarding Qatar.

Jubail is not shown on any map we have as a port. One map shows it as a hill. The town of Qasr-al-Subai is shown as a nearby port.

We did not show Asir because in October, 1926, it accepted the suzerainty of Ibn Sa'ud, and in 1930 under a new arrangement with its titular sovereign, the Idrisi, it was practically annexed to the Hejaz which had itself been conquered by Ibn Sa'ud. Also our material shows that Sabiya was the capital of this principality. This town we have shown.

About the 10,300 foot elevation: This does not apply to San'a but to the tiny dot to the west. The use of a dot to locate an elevation is indicated in our map legend.

We are glad to learn about the development of "Duwadami." Our maps show it as relatively unimportant. We will include it on future maps.

Very truly yours,

Albert H. Bumstead

Albert H. Bumstead
Cartographer

K. S. TWITCHELL.
MINING ENGINEER

Cables;
KARTWITCH,
LONDON.

RECEIVED

522, FIFTH AVENUE.
NEW YORK CITY.

1934 23 AM 9:06

DEPART OF STATE
DIVISION OF
COMMUNICAT RECORDS

Office of the Geographer
APR 20 1934
DEPARTMENT OF STATE

Two maps filed in Office
of the Geographer under nos:
415 Feb   415 Feb.
1934a   1934q

c/o Guaranty Trust Co. of New York,
32, Lombard Street,
London, E.C.3. 890F.937 1

actd t optic d
to Mr Bumstead
4/18/34
PHA/LS

April 3, 1934.

Wallace Murray, Esq.,
Chief of the Division of Near Eastern Affairs
Department of State,
Washington, D.C.

APR 24 1934
DIVISION OF
NEAR EASTERN AFFAIRS

890F.63/3

Dear Mr. Murray;

    I had hoped to have had the pleasure of again
seeing you long before now. I arrived here from Arabia and
the Sudan just before Christmas. Before my departure from Jedda
the King and Government gave me a letter requesting that I interest capital in the development of mines, roads and oil - the
latter in areas not, of course, included in the Eastern Saudi
Arabia oil concession. This time while I was at Riyadh, I
was given permission to interest British and American capital.
The latter is the reason for my delay here. Twice groups have
practically decided to take up the mines development, and then
reconsidered and decided in the negative. At present the mines
are being considered by the American Smelting & Refining Co. -
their representative here having my reports and sending a synopsis to the head office in New York. I have not yet received their
decision. It is all very interesting but I am extremely anxious to return and get the work started as their is so much to be
done.

    I had two extremely interesting visits at Riyadh as guest
of King Ibn Saud during my trips across from the Red Sea to the
Persian Gulf and return last fall. When I see you I shall be
glad to show you the photos I took last year and to give you
any you may wish. I enclose a few which are, perhaps, unique
as I was informed that no photographs are allowed to be taken in
Riyadh. When I asked the king for permission he hesitated and
then directed that I be taken to different places in the palace
to get views, so the enclosed are taken in, and from the royal
palace of a thousand rooms".
No. 2091 - King Abdul Aziz Ibn Saud
" 2094 - The center figure is Shaikh Yussuf Yassin, the Chief
        Secretary, almost a prime minister in the old sense
        of the word. He, Shaikh Abdulla Suleiman (Minister of
        Finance) and Shaikh Fuad Hamza (Acting Minister of
        Foreign Affairs) are the most influential of the king's
        advisors.

No.2088 - View from the palace into the market at Riyadh.

No.2087 - Another view from the palace of one of the markets.
The yellow arrow points to a low minaret. The strict
Wahabis do not approve of the usual tall,graceful minarets
nor domed roofs, so in this Nejd capital minarets are
all low,the buildings are plain and severe. The Spanish
and Mexican patio,or courtyard, is said to have originated
in Nejd. The palaces and buildings I was in were of this
style.

I had several most pleasant talks with the King
during my stays of four and five days in Riyadh. He had done
everything in his power to avert the present war with the Yemen.
He told me of a cable he had received from Mr.C.R.Crane and his
reply relative to this matter.

The immediate occasion of my inflicting this long
letter upon you is the new map of Asia published by the National
Geographic Society. I wrote Mr.Simpich about inaccuracies,he
passed these on to Mr.Bumstead the Cartographer whose letter I enclose as it refers to your Department.   I also enclose the
above mentioned map with the Ruba' -al -Khali boundary as claimed
by King Ibn Saud marked in black ink by the Saudu Arab Minister
in London, Shaikh Hafiz Wahba. He also marked a small space about
Dohah on the Qatar peninsular. Ibn Saud claims this area outside
of Dohah and when the oil geologists of the Anglo Persian Oil Co.
recently attempted to go west they were turned back. If the
British exert force to"protect" Qata,the most western limit
would, I am sure, be a line from Salwa Bay to the western limit of
Khor-adh-Dhuwaihin - all much to the east of the boundary shown
by the National Geographic map. I enclose a 1 : 1,000,000 map
which shows this district well. It also shows the port of Jubail.
"Qasr-al-Subai" is only an abandoned ruin , not a port.
Shaikh Hafiz Wahba also confirmed by statement to the National Geographic Society, that Abha, is the capital of Asir, as the
shown on the map,I am sending you under separate cover, not Sabiya
as shown on the Nat.Geo.Soc.map.
There are Government wireless stations at Jubail,Qatif,Ojair,
Riyadh,Duwadami,Taif,Mecca,Jedda,Rabigh,Yenbo, and Wedj; as well as
other places which I do not know personally.
If any, or all, of this information is of interest and use
to you I shall be very glad.
If you have duplicates of the enclosed maps, or do not wish,
them,please send them on to Mr.Simpich or Mr.Bumstead.
Should I be successful with my present mining negotiations,
or not, please inform me if I can be of service to you in any way
in connection with Arabia.
I apologize for such a long letter.

Yours sincerely,

April 21, 1934

My dear Mr. Bumstead:

I have just received a letter from Mr. K. S. Twitchell,
a geologist who has spent considerable time during the past
few years in Arabia, in which, with reference to your letter
to him of February 20, 1934, regarding Arabian boundaries, he
makes the following comments:

> "The immediate occasion of my inflicting
> this long letter upon you is the new map of
> Asia published by the National Geographic Society.
> I wrote Mr. Simpich about inaccuracies, he passed
> these on to Mr. Bumstead the Cartographer whose
> letter I enclose as it refers to your Department.
> I also enclose the above mentioned map with the
> Ruba' -al -Khali boundary as claimed by King Ibn
> Saud marked in black ink by the Saudi Arab Minister
> in London, Shaikh Hafiz Wahba. He also marked a
> small space about Dohah on the Qatar peninsular.
> Ibn Saud claims this area outside of Dohah and when
> the oil geologists of the Anglo Persian Oil Co.
> recently attempted to go west they were turned
> back. If the British exert force to 'protect'
> Qatar, the most western limit would, I am sure, be
> a line from Salwa Bay to the western limit of Khor-
> adh-Dhuwaihin — all much to the east of the boundary
> shown by the National Geographic map. I enclose a
> 1:1,000,000 map which shows this district well. It
> also shows the port of Jubail. 'Qasr-al-Subai' is
> only an abandoned ruin, not a port.
>
> "Shaikh Hafiz Wahba also confirmed by state-
> ment to the National Geographic Society, that
> Abha is the capital of Asir, as shown on the

map

Mr. Albert H. Bumstead,
    Cartographer,
        National Geographic Society,
            Washington, D.C.

- 2 -

map (1 inch to 32 miles) I am sending you
under separate cover, not Sabiya as shown
on the Nat. Geo. Soc. map.

"There are Government wireless stations
at Jubail, Qatif, Ojair, Riyadh, Duwadami, Taif,
Mecca, Jedda, Rabigh, Yenbo, and Wedj; as well
as other places which I do not know personally."

I am passing this information along to you for what-

ever it may be worth and for such discreet use as you may

wish to make of it. I am also enclosing two of the maps

mentioned in Mr. Twitchell's letter on which he or the

Arabian Minister in London has indicated certain boundaries.

Will you be good enough to return these maps to me when

they have served their purpose?

Sincerely yours,

Wallace Murray,
Chief, Division of Near Eastern Affairs.

Enclosure:

Two maps

[Editor's Note: Two maps mentioned were not included in Archive's files.]

SAUDI ARABIAN MINING SYNDICATE, LIMITED.

DIRECTORS:
LOUIS HARDY.
Alternate G. H. HUTTON (U.S.A.)
H. R. EDWARDS (U.S.A.)
E. D. McDERMOTT.

MANAGER:
K. S. TWITCHELL.

RECEIVED
DEPARTMENT OF STATE

IN REPLY PLEASE QUOTE

1934 AUG 6 PM 2 52

DIVISION OF
COMMUNICATIONS
AND RECORDS
AUG 7 1934
DIVISION OF
NEAR EASTERN AFFAIRS

Djedda,
Hedjaz,
Saudi, Arabia.

NE-PNA-

August 10 1934.

July 8, 1934.

890F.63/4

FILED

Wallace Murray, Esq.,
Chief of Division of Near Eastern Affairs,
Department of State,
Washington, D.C.

Dear Mr. Murray;

I wish to thank you very much for your letters
April 21st and May 8th. I am glad the maps were useful to
you.

I thank you very much for taking up the matter
of archaeological research in Arabia. I have read with
interest the letters you have received regarding this matter.
I shall send the latter three on to a friend of mine in New
York who has expressed an interest and who will get into
touch with Harvard, Princeton, Michigan and Pennsylvania when
the time is auspicious. (He is Everard C. Stokes, Vice-Pre-
sident of The Church Properties Fire Insurance Corp., 22 William St., New York.)

I shall mention this matter to the Acting Minister
of Foreign Affairs (Shaikh Yussuff Yassin) and to King Ibn
Saud when I meet them, in order to make certain that Shaikh
Hafiz Wahba had their approval when he asked me to take up
this matter. I arrived here a few days ago. It may be of
general interest to you to know that Shaikh Fuad Hamza, the
Deputy Minister of Foreign Affairs, has left by steamer today
on an enforced leave of absence to regain his health. He has
recently had severe heart attacks.

The Emir Feisal is still at Jizan, Asir, organiz-
ing and establishing government in that recently fought over
country. He is expected back here within a month.

A Mission of Peace from Ethiopia, which you know
has been visiting the Yemen, landed here last week and is now
with Ibn Saud and Govt. at their summer capital at Taif.
Strange to say one member, David Hall, is an old acquaintance
whom I knew then I was in Addis Ababa in 1926 and 1927.

SAUDI ARABIAN MINING SYNDICATE, LIMITED.

DIRECTORS:
LOUIS HARDY.
Alternate G. H. HUTTON (U.S.A.)
H. R. EDWARDS (U.S.A.)
E. D. McDERMOTT.

MANAGER:
K. S. TWITCHELL.

IN REPLY PLEASE QUOTE

Djedda,

Hedjaz,

Saudi, Arabia.

The Minister of Finance, Shaikh Abdulla Suleiman, who has been with the Saudi Army in Hodeidah, is expected back here tomorrow.

I think this is all the Saudi news.

Personally I am here to endeavour to negotiate with this Government for an agreement with my syndicate to develop the mineral resources - or some of them - of this country. Whether or not I shall be successful, it is impossible to say yet.

If conditions are agreed, our plan is to make an exte extensive examination of the most attractive parts of the north-western part of this country, do a certain amount of development; and if results are sufficiently favorable, form companies for the actual mining of the properties which warrant it.

I am enclosing a statement by The Guaranty Trust Co. of New York, 32 Lombard St., London, as to the standing of the members of the Syndicate. I think you will agree that I have been extremely fortunate in securing such a group of leading mining men. It has not been easy for I have had five American and four British companies refuse to go into this matter; once started, however, several of them have become members of the Syndicate. It was considerably oversubscribed; I was told in London that it is a uniquely representative mining group. Last December I terminated my engagement with the Standard Oil Co. of California, so was free to take up the problem of the development of mines.

If successfull in securing an agreement, the mining work would include a certain amount of archaeological as we should concentrate our operations on the clearing and examination of ancient mines. If you are interested I shall keep you informed of developments. I shall appreciate your remarks.

Kindest regards and many thanks for your interest.

Yours sincerely,

K.S.Twitchell

GERALD H.HUTTON. 55/61, Moorgate E.C.2.

Gerald Hillsdon Hutton is General Manager and a director of Anglo-Oriental
(Malaya) Ltd., Ipoh, Federated Malay States, and is also on the board of
the following companies, all at 55/61, Moorgate, E.C. 2:

Anglo-Malayan Tin Ltd.
Associated Tin (Malaya) Ltd.
Changkat Tin Dredging Ltd.
Jelapang Tin Dredging Ltd
Kampong Lunjut Tin Dredging Ltd.
Kramat Tin Dredging Ltd.
Kuala Kampar Tin Fields Ltd.
Kundang Tin Dredging Ltd.
Lower Perak Tin Dredging Ltd.
Malim Nawar Tin Ltd.
Rawang Tin Fields Ltd
Southern Kampar Tin Dredging Ltd
Tanah Biji Ltd.

Hutton is spoken of as a respectable, capable man, is of American nationality,
and a Mining Engineer by profession.

He is believed to be possessed of means, has hitherto fulfilled his undertakings, and those approached express the opinion that Hutton would not
be likely to wittingly enter into engagements beyond his capacity.

....

G. GOLDTHORP HAY. 56/61, Moorgate, E.C.

Subject of report who is well known in mining circles, is reported to be
interested in several well known and important companies and holds the
position of director with the following:-

Lake View & Star Ltd. (Managing Director)
Anglo-Maikop Corpn. Ltd (Director)
Barrier South Ltd (Director)
Brixworth Ironstone Co. Ltd. (Director)
Maikop Pipeline & Transport Co Ltd.
Mill-close Mines Ltd. (Director)
Venture Trust Ltd.
Yukon Consolidated Gold Corpn. Ltd.

Hay is regarded as a respectable, capable man, and so far as we can hear,
has hitherto proved satisfactory in his dealings. Authorities consulted
regard him as good for his reasonable engagements.

....

LOUIS HARDY. Lloyds Bank Buildings, Moorgate: E.C.

Hardy, who resides privately at the Pines, Bexley, Kent, is Chairman of
the Anglo-Oriental & General Investment Trust Ltd. Parkanchy Tin Ltd.,
Polhigey Tin Ltd. and Wheal Kitty Tin Ltd. and is also a director of
the following companies:-

Anglo-Oriental Mining Corpn. Ltd.   Johore River Rubber Plantations Ltd.
Juga Valley Tin Areas Ltd.   Junction Tin Mine (Nigeria) Ltd.
Kampar Malaya Tin Dredging Ltd.   London Lubricants Ltd.
London Nigerian Power Co. Ltd   Lyndhurst Deep Level (Gold & Silver)Ld.
Maiangwa Tin Mines Ltd.   Malayan Tinfields Ltd.
Nanette Rubber Plantations Ltd.   New Goldfields of Venezuela Ltd.
North Malay Rubber Estates Ltd.   Talerng Tin Dredging Ltd.
Tavoy Tin Dredging Corpn. Ltd.

The companies mentioned are in good repute and Hardy is regarded as a
respectable,capable man. He is believed to be in a good financial position,
has hitherto met his engagements, and parties consulted express the opinion
that he would not be likely to enter into undertakings he could not see his
way to fulfill.

D.P. MITCHELL, Mining Engineer, Adelaide House, King William St. E.C.

Deane Prescott Mitchell is an American Mining Engineer and is spoken of as a respectable man of good reputation. He is believed to be in satisfactory general circumstances and is interested in the following undertakings:

1. Mining Trust Ltd. of the above address, a large and important company which was formed to acquire non-Russian interests of Russo-Asiatic Consolidated Ltd. and other assets, and to acquire and hold shares, stocks, debentures, debenture stocks, bonds etc. In addition to which there are several subsidiary mining companies. Of the undertaking, Mitchell is a director.

2. Mitchell is a director of New Guinea Goldfields Ltd. whose London office is situated at the above mentioned address. New Guinea Goldfields Ltd. is a large and important Company.

3. As a director he also appears on the board of Russo-Asiatic Consolidated Ltd. of Adelaide House, King William St. E.C. 4.

    Mitchell who holds the degree of M.A.I.M.E. is believed to reside privately at 3, Melbury Road, Kensington, W.14.

....

Rt. Hon. The Earl Castle Stewart M.C., M.P. Old Lodge, Uckfield, Sussex.

Subject of enquiry who is the seventh Earl, was born in August 1889, and in 1920 married Eleanor May, daughter of H.S. Guggenheim of New York. In addition to his residence at the address given, he is also of Stuart Hall, Stewartstown Co. Tyrone.

He is well spoken of and is believed in good circumstances.
He is Chairman of the Mining Trust Ltd. a large and important company which was formed to acquire non-Russian interests of Russo-Asiatic Consolidated Ltd. and other assets and to acquire and hold shares, stocks, debentures, debenture stocks, bonds etc. In addition to which there are several subsidiary mining companies.

He is also on the London Board of the Lautaro Nitrate Co. Ltd.

....

WALTER McDERMOTT, Mining Engineer, 2a, Guildhall Chambers, Basinghall St E.C.

Subject of enquiry is a mining engineer practising from the above address, and is well known.
He holds appointments in several important undertakings among which are the following:-

Anglo American Corporation of South Africa Ltd. (director & London agent)
Buena Tierra Mining Co. Ltd. (Director)
Consolidated Mines Selection Co. Ltd. (Chairman)
Fresnillo Company (London committee)
Mexican Corporation Ltd. (Director)
Rhodesian Anglo American Ltd. (Director)
Rhodesian Land, Cattle & Ranching Corp. Ltd. (London Committee)
West Springs Ltd (London Committee)

He is of good reputation and standing in the mining world and looked upon as trustworthy and reliable, for his undertakings.
McDermott who holds the following degrees M. Inst.M.M., M.A.I.M.E., is understood to reside privately at 115, Church St. Chelsea, S.W. 3.

E.D.McDERMOTT. 5, London Wall Buildings, E.C.2.

Edward Duffield Mc Dermott M. Inst. M.M. is understood to be residing
privately at "The Dene", Borough Green, Sevenoaks, and is spoken of as a
respectable man. He is a director of Consolidated Mines Selection Co. Ltd.
which is a large and important company with a capital of £600,000.
He is a mining engineer and a son of Walter McDermott who is Chairman of
the above mentioned company and also of the same profession.

Subject of report is regarded as a respectable and capable man, who appears
to have hitherto been satisfactory in his dealings and is not thought
likely to undertake liabilities he could not satisfactorily discharge.

....

H. ROBERT EDWARDS, 55/61, Moorgate, E.C. 2.

Hugh Robert Edwards, M.Inst.M.M., M.A.I.M.E., is an American engineer and
holds several important appointments among which is that of Executive
Engineer to the Anglo-Oriental Mining Corpn. Ltd. of the above address.
He is also a director of the following companies:-

Barium Consolidated Ltd.,	Kenongo Gold Mines Ltd
Lyndhurst Deep Level (Gold & Silver) Ltd.	Mawchi Mines Ltd
New Goldfields of Venezuela Ltd.	Parkanchy Tin Ltd
Polhigey Tin Ltd.	Wheal Kitty Tin Ltd.

He is a well-known man, is regarded as respectable and capable and is
understood to be residing privately at Chateau de Madrid, Northwood, Middx.
As far as known he has hitherto met his engagements, is believed in satisfactory circumstances and is not thought likely to entertain transactions
he could not fulfill.

....

PERCY MARMION, 95 Gresham St., E.C. 2.

Subject of report, who is well known, is spoken of as a highly respectable
man, and is considered trustworthy for his engagements. He is Vice-Chairman
and Joint Managing Director of the Burma Corpn. Ltd. of the above mentioned
address, which is an important company owing zinc, lead, silver and copper
mines, situated in the Federated Shan States of Upper Burma and various
other leasehold mining and other property.
Marmion is also Vice-Chairman of the British Non-Ferrous Mining Corpn. Ltd.
of 73/76, King William St. E.C. 4. which is an important company dealing with
non-ferrous mining properties. As a director he also appears on the board
of the Imperial Smelting Corpn. Ltd. which is a large and important undertaking with offices at 95, Gresham St. E.C.2. He is believed to be residing
privately at Firlands, Reigate Road, Reigate, Surrey.

....

CHARLES A. BANKS. 19, St Swithin's Lane, E.C.

Banks is a Consulting Mining Engineer by profession and a Member of the
Institute of Mining and Metallurgy, is an American, and his headquarters
areat 612, Pacific Buildings, Hastings Street, West, Vancouver, B.C.
He is managing director in Canada of British Canadian Silver Corpn. Ltd.
managing director of Bulolo Gold Dredging Ltd, and managing director of
Placer Development Ltd. Banks is regarded as a respectable, capable man,
is not thought to be without means and so far as we can hear has hitherto
proved satisfactory in his dealings. Authorities consulted consider him
good for his engagements.
The address, 19, St Swithin's lane, is that of the Secretary and Offices
of the British Canadian Silver Corpn. Ltd.

116

H.S. MUNROE, 13/14, Austin Friars, E.C.

Harold S. Munroe who is an American mining engineer, is a director of Rhokana Corpn. Ltd. of the above mentioned address.

The Company mentioned above, is a large and important undertaking with exclusive prospecting rights in South Africa.

It is understood that subject of report as a mining engineer is closely associated with Chester Beatty, a well known and important figure in the mining world, and as such it is believed that he is at present in charge in Rhodesia.

Subject of report is regarded as respectable and of good standing. His residence is understood to be N'Kana, North Rhodesia.

•••••••••••••••

CARL LINDBERG. 49, Moorgate, London, E.C.

Carl O. Lindberg, of American nationality, is a well known American Mining Engineer, having his offices at 70, Pine Street, New York, U.S.A.

He is Vice President of the American Potash & Chemical Corporation, also Vice President of the botanamo mining Corporation, is on the American Advisory Committee of Goldfields American Development Co. Ltd. and on the American Advisory Committee of the New Consolidated Gold Fields Ltd. and a director of Placer Development Ltd.

Lindberg is described as a very respectable and well connected man, who would seem to be in a satisfactory financial position and so far as we can hear has hitherto duly discharged his obligations.

In quarters where enquiries have been made the opinion is expressed that he would not wittingly enter into undertakings he could not see his way to satisfactorily discharge.

Lindberg is a Member of the Institute of Mining and Metallurgy.

The address quoted, 49 Moorgate, E.C. is that of the Goldfields American Development Co Ltd.

W. HAROLD EDWARDS. 55/61, Moorgate, E.C.

William Harold Edwards is a Member of the London Committee of the Northern Transvall (Messina) Copper Exploration Ltd., a member of the Council of the Tin Producers Association and the Nigerian Chamber of Mines, and is also on the board of the following companies:-

Ampat Tin Dredging Ltd.
Associated Tin (Malaya) Ltd
Indo-General Corpn (Malay) Ltd.
Kampar Malaya Tin Dredging Ltd.
London African Tin Syndicate Ltd.
London Bolvian Tin Syndicate Ltd.
London Tin Corporation Ltd.
Lower Perak Tin Dredging Ltd.
Polhigey Tin Ltd.
Southern Kampar Tin Dredging Ltd.
Southern Siamese Tin Dredging Ltd.
Talerng Tin Dredging Ltd.
Tavoy Prospectors Ltd.
Tavoy Tin Dredging Corpn. Ltd.
Toyo Tin Ltd.
EDWARDS is well known in London commercial circles, is a respectable, capable man, and resides in good style, having an address at 20, Farm Street, W.1. and also Stone House, Bucks. He is believed to be in a sound financial position, duly meets his obligations, and considered good for his engagements by those consulted.

DONALD McFARLANE, Dock House, Billiter Street, LONDON. E.C.

Donald McFarlane was formerly a Director of Gellatley, Hankey & Co, (Sudan) Ltd., which was registered in the Sudan as a limited liability company with nominal capital of £100.000. He left that Company and is now associated with the London Company, Gellatly Hankey & Co Ltd. of Dock House, Billiter Street, E.C., Steamship Owners and Brokers, a' private company registered in 1927 with £ 100,000 capital all issued. McFarlane is spoken of as a respectable man and whilst the actual extent of his means have not transpired, those consulted consider that he would be unlikely to undertake obligations beyond his capacity to fulfill.

....

August 10 1934.

In reply refer to
NE 890F.63/4

890F.63/4

Dear Mr. Twitchell:

I was much interested in your letter of July 8, 1934, telling me of the plans of the Saudi Arabian Mining Syndicate, Limited, and of its organization. Both from a personal and an official point of view I am interested how the new venture is progressing.

Among the members of the Syndicate listed on the papers which you sent me, I noticed the names of six Americans and eight Britishers.   The Syndicate itself is, of course, a British limited company and I wondered whether the majority of control was also in British hands. If you feel free to enlighten me on this point it would be useful information to have on hand, for we are naturally interested in learning just how extensive American interests in Saudi Arabia are or are likely to become.

I shall look forward to hearing from you again and

in

Mr. K. S. Twitchell,
        Manager, Saudi Arabian Mining
                Syndicate, Limited,
                    Djedda,
                        Hedjaz,
                            Saudi, Arabia.

- 2 -

in the meantime I wish you the best of fortune in
your new undertaking.

Sincerely yours,

Wallace Murray,
Chief, Division of Near Eastern Affairs.

NE PHA/GO

K.S.Twitchell,
Jedda,
Hedjaz,
Saudi Arabia.

November 14 1934

Written from;
Taif, the summer capital
of Hedjaz,Elev.5,200 ft.

890F.63/6

October 15,1934.
Rajab 4,1353.

Wallace Murray,Esq.,Chief,
Division of the Near East,
State Department,
Washington, D.C.

Dear Mr.Murray;

          I was very glad to receive your letter of
August 10th, a month ago.   I have been delaying my reply in
hopes that I might inform you that the Minies Concession had
been signed.   Agreement has been reached on all except one
point, which is a minor one, so I am in hopes that within a
few days the documents will be sent to Riyadh for the King's
final approval and that I may sign here by the first of November.   But the delays have been agravating .   I have run out
of stationery - as you may see- as well as patience,almost.

          The Syndicate is controlled by British subjects al-
though there is a large American interest in it.   Eight
different American companies refused to go into this venture
as well as four British before I was able to arrange a
British Company -in which I have both American and British
friends -   to take the initiative in forming the Syndicate.
Once statted most of those who had previously refused to go
into this matter joined the Syndicate, besides others, and it
was oversubscribed.

          If you would wish details of the terms of the Concession
with the Saudi Arab Govt. I shall be glad to give them to you,-
of course, with the approval the Directors of the Syndicate.
If signed , the Concession will be published in Mecca by the
Govt. newspaper,so I am sure you will be welcome to all such
information if you so desire. The terms are exceedingly favorable to the Govt. as they have a participation in each company
to be formed as well as royalties and land rentals. The area
concerned is about 240,000 square miles and the time similar
to the oil concession.

          Again I thank you for your good wishes.
                Yours sincerely,
                K.S.Twitchell

SAUDI ARABIAN MINING SYNDICATE, LIMITED

DIRECTORS
LOUIS HARDY.
Alternate G. H. HUTTON (U.S.A.
H. R. EDWARDS (U.S.A.)
E. D. McDERMOTT.

MANAGER
K. S. TWITCHELL.

IN REPLY PLEASE QUOTE

Jiddah, Yenbo,

Hejaz,

Saudi Arabia.

March IIth. 1935

Wallace Murray Esq.,
Chief of Near Eastern Affairs,
Department Of State.
Washington. D.C.

Dear Mr. Murray,

I have been delaying in answering your letter of
Nov. 14th. as the signing of the Concession was delayed longer than
anticipated. The final formalities were completed on Dec. 24th. and
the Concession ratified by my Syndicate on Jan.IIth. in London. The
effective date of the contract is Feb.15th, 1935, being the date of
its publication in the official newspapers in Mecca. I have commun-
icated with the Directors who have given permission to send you the
concession documents as you requested.

Under separate cover I take pleasure in mailing
you both the Arabic and English texts.

It may interest you to know that the area involved
is approximately 120,000 square miles, or the size of all the
British Isles. Should there be any questions or information that
you wish to know, I should be only too glad to give you such.

I may say that we have started already on drilling
one of the possible "placer" properties and are starting the examin-

- 2 -

-ation of two loade properties next week.

Kindest regards,

Yours sincerely.

K.S. Twitchell

<u>DATED 17th. RAMADAN 1353 (23rd. December 1934)</u>

THE SAUDI ARABIAN GOVERNMENT

- and -

SAUDI ARABIAN MINING SYNDICATE
LIMITED.

————————

A G R E E M E N T
for prospecting Mining Concession.

————————

124

MINING CONCESSION FROM THE SAUDI ARABIAN GOVERNMENT TO THE SAUDI ARABIAN MINING SYNDICATE LIMITED.

This agreement made the I7th. day of Ramadan I353 a.h. being the 23rd. day of December I934 A.D. between SHEIKH ABDULLAH SULEIMAN AL HAMDAN, Minister of Finance of Saudi Arabia, acting on behalf of the Saudi Arabian Government (Hereinafter referred to as"the Government") of the one part and KARL SABEN TWITCHELL acting on behalf of the Saudi Arabian Mining Syndicate Limited whose registered office is situated at 55/6I Moorgate in the City of London, England (hereinafter referred a to as " The Syndicate") of the other part.

It is herby agreed between the Government and the Syndicate in the manner following:-

ARTICLE I.
CONCESSION
(A) The Government hereby grants to the Syndicate, on the terms and conditions hereinafter set forth, the exclusive right to search for explore and prospect on and under the land of the region delineated in article two hereunder for minerals and metals and for that purpose to make cuttings, shafts, excavations and tunnels and to bore thereon and thereunder together with the right to all possible and neccessary facilities as contained in this agreement for the accomplishment of purposes aforesaid for a period of two years from the effective date of this agreement.

ARTICLE 2
AREA
The area covered by the exclusive right referred to in Article one hereof is shown on the sketch map attached as exibit "A" and it's boundaries are as follows:- Commencing from the North East at a point of longtitude 38 East and latitude 29o - 35o North, from there Westerly to the end of the boundaries of the territory which is at present under the administration of the Government of Saudi Arabia, along the Transjordan frontier; on the West the boundary is the Gulf of Aqaba and the Red Sea extending southerly to Khor Al Birk at Latitude I8o -IO' North; thence North Easterly to the village of Raghdan in Ghamith; thence North Westerly to Barth Samuda, from there Northerly to Eshaira, from Eshaira North Easterly to Al Mahdatha, Al Kharaba, and Maran to Iqbah which is water at the boundaries of Kushb on it's Western side; from Iqbah which is water at the boundaries of Kushb on it's Western side from Iqbah in a straight line to Mahad Dahab which is considered at about 20 kilometres Easterly fromm Jiraisiyah; from here in a straight line North Westerly to Hanakiya; thence in a straight line to Hadiya station on the Hedjaz Railway leaving Khairbar outside of the concession area; from Hadiya in a straight line North Westerly to the intersecting point of Longtitude 38o East and Latitude 29o - 35' North.

Page Two

It is understood that the following shall be excluded from the concession area:-

Medina and it's boundaries which shall not exceed thirty kilometres from the walls of that City.

And furthermore the sacred area of Mecca whose boundaries are from Sadiya on the South, to Al Sail on the East, and thence to Asfan on the North West, and thence Southerly through Bahra back to Sadiya.

ARTICLE 3

PROGRAMME.

(A)   The work of exploration and/or prospecting on the whole area under the Concession shall commence within a period of three months from the effective date of this agreement and shall be prosecuted continuously unless prevented by force majeure. Prospecting Equipment shall be ordered by the Syndicate within thirty days of the effective date of the agreement.

(B)   On or before the expiration of one year from the effective date of the agreement , the Syndicate shall select areas and places within the region which it desires to explore and prospect further.

The Syndicate shall establish an office in Jeddah at the expiration of the first year from the effective date of this agreement.

(C)   On or before the expiration of two years from the effective date of the agreement, the Syndicate shall select lands and places which it desires to lease for a period of fifty eight years from the date of the grant of the lease, or leases, with a view to conducting active mining operations by means of an operating company or companies to be formed by the Syndicate.

ARTICLE 4

RENTALS AND PAYMENTS.

(A)   The Syndicate shall pay no ground rental to the Government during the first year described in Article Three (A).

(B)   The Syndicate shall pay to the Government yearly in advance during the second prospecting year ground rentals at the rate of four shillings sterling per acre (the acre is 4047 metres) for lands selected for further prospecting under Article Three (B).

(C)   The Syndicate shall pay to the Government yearly in advance ground rentals at the rate of One Pound sterling per acre for lands selected under Article Three (C).

126

(D)   The Syndicate shall also pay to the Government during the prospecting period five per cent of the gross value of the production, or the land rentals of four shilling sterling per acre , whichever shall be the greater.

(E)   All payments shall be made in such currency and to such Bank as the Government shall specify, at the prevailing rates of exchange at the date of payment.

(F)   The Syndicate before assigning it's rights to any other company for the developement of any area shall notify the Government and obtain it's approval - it being understood that the Government shall not withhold such approval without grave and sufficient reasons which it considers injutious to it's interests.

ARTICLE 5

GOVEMENT OBLIGATIONS.

      The Government further undertakes as follows:-
(A)   To grant to the Syndicate or it's successors or assigns a lease, or leases, in the form of Exibit "B" attached hereto upon application by the Syndicate, as set forth under Article Three "C".

(B)   The Government shall undertake to protect the Syndicate, it's employees, the properties; the form of such protection shall be described in detail in special letters which shall be exchanged between the Government and the Syndicate and shall be subject to modification from time to time as conditions shall vary. It being understood that the Syndicate shall pay direct to the Government the wages of such guards as shall be agreed.

(C)   To exempt the Syndicate and it's successors in interest from all direct and indirect taxes, imposts, charges, fees, and export duties on minerals, metals and bullion produced, but the Syndicate shall pay the Government a custom's duty of ten per cent of the certified invoice valuation of all it's imports, it being understood that the Syndicate shall not sell within the Kingdom any such imported products until the Customs Duties paid by others shall have been paid on such products, it being further understood that the above certification shall be made by a Chamber of Commerce, Saudi Legation, or in the absence of these by a responsible authority such as a notaryPublic, Court, or Government Department.

(D)   To give the Syndicate the right to use all means and facilities that may be deemed neccessary or advisable in order to carry out the purposes of the enterprises, including among other things the right to construct and use roads, camps, buildings, structures, and all systems of communications, to install and operate machinery, equipment and facilities in connection with exploration and prospecting

or in connection with the transportation, storeage, treatment,
manufacture or dealing with the exportation of metals or minerals,
or in connection with the camps, buildings and quarters of the
personell of the Syndicate, to construct and use storeage, resevoirs,
tanks, bins, and receptacles, to construct and operate wharves, piers,
sea loading lines, bins and lighters, and to use all forms of transportation for personnel or equipment and all ores, minerals and
products.

It is understood, however, that the use of aeroplanes and wireless
within the country shall be the subject of a separate agreement.

It is also understood that the Government shall be allowed to
use railway, road and port facilities established by the Syndicate
so long as such use shall not interfere with the operations of the
Syndicate. The form of such use shall be the subject of a separate
agreement at the time of need.

(E) To give the Syndicate the right to develop, carry away and use
water, and also to carry away and use any water belonging to the
Government for the operation of the enterprise, but not so as to
prejudice irrigation or deprive any lands, houses, or watering places
for cattle of a reasonable supply of water from time to time.

(F) To give the Syndicate the right to take and use, but only to the
extent neccessary for the purposes of the enterprise, other natural
products belonging to the Government, such as surface soil, stone,
lime, gypsum and similar substances, also timber and wood for domestic
purposes but not for the power or construction.

(G) In times of serious emergency to compensate the Syndicate for
any use by the Government of the Syndicate's transportation and
communication facilities, for any loss which may be sustained by the
Syndicate thereby, whether through damage to the Syndicate's facilities,
equipment or operation, it being understood that the Government shall
not compensate the Syndicate for it's estimated profits during the perie
period of such emergency use. Furthermore, the Government shall not be
under obligation to compensate the Syndicate for any damage or injury
occurring through force majeure.

(H) To empower the Syndicate to acquire any owner or occupant the
surface rights of any land which shall be deemed neccessary to use
in connection with the work of prospecting and exploration, or mining
operations, provided that the owner or occupant shall be paid for the
use of such lands or land. The payment shall be equitable having regard
to the customary use made of the land by the owner or occupant, plus
reasonable profits. The Government will operate with the Syndicate
in the event of any difficulties arising with respect to the acquisition
of such rights from a surface occupant or owner.

128

ARTICLE 6

SYNDICATE OBLIGATIONS

The Syndicate further agrees and undertakes as follows:-
(A) It shall not conduct work in, or occupy, any religious or sacred area, such as cemeteries, mosques etc.

(B) It shall give the duly authorized representative of the Government, during the usual hours of operation, full facilities and access to all it's operations and records for the purpose of inspecting the work carried on by the Syndicate .

(C) It's employees shall not interfere with the administrative, political, or religious affairs within Saudi Arabia. The penalty of breach of this provision will be deportation of the employee so offending and after such employee shall been punished according to the laws of the country and shall have paid the customary indemnity usual for such offence, it being understood that the laws and regulations of Saudi Arabia shall apply to all employees of the Syndicate in the same way as they apply to others residing in the country.

(D) All it's operations shall be directed and supervised by personnel appointed by the Syndicate who shall employ Saudi Arab nationals as far as practicable. They will not employ other nationals as long as competent Saudi Arab nationals are available for such work. It being understood that foreign subjects of adjacent countries who shall be employed by the Syndicate - by reason of lack of nationals competent for such services - it shall submit to the Government their names and identities prior to their definite appointment. If the Government does not object within a period of one month the Syndicate shall consider that the Government has given it's approval for their employment.

All contracts with Saudi Arab subjects involving a time exceeding one month shall be submitted to the Government for it's advice and approval, if the Syndicate does not recieve an adverse reply from the Government within fifteen days from the date of telegraphing such notice the approval shall be deemed as given.
(E)
(E) It shall abide by the existing and future laws of Saudi Arabia applicable generally to workers in similar industrial enterprises within the Kingdom.

(F) It shall supply the Government with copies of all/general maps and reports written in connection with operations with reference to the exploration and prospecting and mine operations of the areas governed by this agreement.

Page Six

(G) It shall furnish the Government, for it's confidential reference, within six months after the end of each semeater, a report of the operations under this agreement during the preceding semeater.

(H) It shall give Government officials and agents and personnel an official business the right to use such communication and transportation facilities as the Syndicate and Companies may establish, provided that such use shall not obstruct or interfere with the Syndicate's operations hereunder or not to impose upon it anya undue burden or expense.

(I) Upon the granting of leases under the terms of Articles Three (C) and Five (A) described above, and as soon as it considers that the data obtained so justify, it will in its absolute discretion organize one or more Companies to operate any properties which it deems advisable to equip with mining, milling and extraction equipment, and will formally allot to the Government as part of the consideration for the granting of the lease fifteen per cent of the nominal capital of the said Company or Companies in fully paid shares and said operating Company or Companies shall undertake to comply with the terms of the form of lease as set forth under Exibit "B".

The Syndicate shall offer Arabian Nationals , subject to acceptance within thirty days after due notice to the Government, the privilege of subscribing ten per cent of the subscription offered to the general public in such operating Company or Companies.

Such Company or Companies shall prosecute the work so as to reach commercial production at the earliest possible date consistent with sound mining practice. Mining operations shall include the ordering and shipping of materials and equipment to Saudi Arabia, prospecting, mining, development, constructing of roads, camps, buildings, structures, communication facilities, the installation and operating of machinery, and of facilities for drilling; (drilling may be diamond drilling, churn drilling, rotary drilling,) as well as underground workings, for the purpose of obtaining geological and mining information as well as for water and other substances.

(J) The said lease or leases shall contain a provision that the operating Company or Companies shall from the date of the granting of the lease or leases pay to the Government by half yearly instalments a royalty equal to five per cent of the gross value of the minerals or metals recovered. From the time of granting such lease or leases the prospecting royalties of five per cent under Article Four (D) hereof cease to be payable.

ARTICLE 7

CANCELLATION

(A) This agreement shall be subject to cancellation by the Government

Page Seven

if the Syndicate shall (unless through force majeure) suspend all
work in Saudi Arabia for a period of more than three months, in which
event it shall notify the Syndicate in writing, or by telegram or
cablegram. The Syndicate shall be considered to have suspended it's
operations if it shall not be represented by a person duly authorized in Saudi Arabia for a continous period of three months.

(B) The Syndicate shall have the right to suspend it's operations
on any or all areas which it may have been examining, upon giving
the Government thirty days notice in writing or by telegram or
cablegram which shall be confirmed promptly by letter, but operations
should not under any circumstances, except by force majeure, be
suspended for more than three months, but if they are then, the
Government shall have the right to cancel this agreement, as per
item (A) of this Article, pertaining to said area or areas.

(C) On cancellation of the contract by reason of such notice or from
any other cause, the Syndicate shall thereafter be free of all
further obligations under this agreement except as follows:-
(I) The Syndicate's immovable property, such as roads, wateror other
wells with thier casings, permanent buildings, structures etc. shall
become the property of the Government free of all charges.
(2) The Syndicate shall offer it's movable property in Saudi Arabia
to the Government at a fair price equal to the replacement value of
such property at the time, less depreciation. If the Government does
not accept this offer within thirty days after the termination of this
agreement the Syndicate shall then be required to remove such property
within a period of six months, and any property or any part of it not
so removed shall automatically become the property of the Government
free of all charges.

ARTICLE 8

GENERAL CONDITIONS

(A) The Memorandum and Articles of Association of the Company apply-
ing to Saudi Arabia shall be such as not to interfere with the existing laws of the Kingdom.

(B) CALENDAR. The periods _at times_ referred to in this agreement shall be r
reckoned on the basis of the solar calandar .

(C) LANGUAHE This agreement has been drawn up in Arabic and in
English and both texts shall have equal value.

(D) FORCE MAJEURE. No failure or omission on the part of the
Syndicate to carry out or conform to any of the terms or conditions
of this agreement shall give the Government any claim against the
Syndicate, or be deemed a breach of this agreement, in so far as such
failure or omission may arise from force majeure. If through force

<u>Page Eight</u>

majeure the fulfilment of any term or condition of this agreement
shall be delayed, the period of such delay together with such period
as may be required for the restoration of any damage done through
such delay, shall be added to the terms or periods fixed in this agreement.

(E) <u>ARBITRATION</u>.   If any doubt, difference or dispute shall arise
between the Government and the Syndicate concerning the interpretation
or execution of this agreement or anything herein contained or in
connection herewith or the rights and liabilities of the parties hereunder, it shall, failing any agreement to settle it in any other way,
be referred to two arbitrators, one of whom shall be chosen by each
party, and a referee who shall be chosen by the arbitrators before
proceeding to arbitration. Each party shall nominate it's arbitrator
within thirty days of being requested in writing by the other party to
do so. In the event of the arbitrators failing to agree upon a referee,
the Government and the Syndicate shall in agreement appoint a referee,
and in the event of their failing to agree they shall request the
President of The Permanent Court of International Justice to appoint
a referee. The decision of the arbitrators, or in the case of a difference of opinion between them, the decision of the referee shall be final.
The place of arbitration shall be such as may be agreed upon by the
parties, and in default of agreement shall be the Hague, Holland.

(F) <u>RATIFICATION</u>. It is understood that this agreement after being
signed in Saudi Arabia, shall be subject to ratification by the
Syndicate at it's offices in London(England) before it shall become
effective. After both texts of this agreement have been signed in
duplicate in Saudi Arabia, the signed copies shall be sent by registered
mail in the next outgoing mail to the Syndicate in London (England)
and within ten days after receipt in London the Syndicate shall transmit
to the Government by cable or telegram whether or not it ratifies this
agreement. If the agreement is not ratified by the Syndicate within
ten daysafter receipt of the document in London (England) it shall be
nul and void and of no further force or effect.

Upon ratification of this agreement by the Syndicate, one signed
copy of each text, together with the neccessary evidence as to ratification by the Syndicate, shall be returned to the Government.

Also, upon ratification of this agreement by the Syndicate, it shall
be published in Saudi Arabia in the usual manner by the Government. It
is agreed that the date of such publication shall be effective date
of the agreement.

(G) <u>NOTICES</u>. Any notices required under this agreement shall in the
case of the Government be addressed to the Finance Minister at Mecca
and in the case of the Syndicate shall be addressed to the Authorized
Representative of the Syndicate in Jeddah, it being understood that
such notices shall be addressed during the first year to Mr.K.S.Twitchell

132

or his substitute, in Saudi Arabia, thereafter to the office in Jeddah. Every notice shall be considered as effective from the date of it's delivery to the said office and all notices shall be sent by prepaid registered post.

(H) <u>ASSIGNMENT</u> The Syndicate shall have the right, after securing the approval of the Government, to assign this agreement, and the benefits thereof shall imure to the benefit of the Syndicate it's successors and assigns and any company or companies formed for the purpose of aquiring and operating the properties herein contained.

As witness the hands of Abdullah Suleiman Al Hamdan for and on behalf of the Government and Karl Saben Twitchell for and on behalf of the Syndicate the day and year first before written.

<u>Signed</u>
for and behalf of the)
Saudi Arab Government)...

<u>Signed</u>
for and on behalf of Saudi Arabian)
Mining Syndicate Limited.   ) ....

DATED 17th. RAMADAN 1353 (23rd. DECEMBER 1934)

THE SAUDI ARABIAN GOVERNMENT

- to -

SAUDI ARABIAN MINING SYNDICATE

LIMITED.

_____

MINING LEASE

_____

EXHIBIT "B".

EXHIBIT "B"

MINING LEASE.

This contract made on the .... day of ....
19... BETWEEN THE SAUDI ARAB GOVERNMENT acting by the MINISTER
OF FINANCE of Saudi Arabia for the time being (hereinafter referred to as "The Lessors") of the one part and the SAUDI
ARABIAN MINING SYNDICATE LIMITED whose Registered Office is
situate at 55/61 Moorgate in the City of London (England)
(hereinafter referred to as "The Lessees")

WITNESSETH as follows: -

1.   The Lessors hereby demise unto the Lessees all and
every the metals and minerals of every description whatso-
ever (except oil shales and mineral oil) (all of which are
included in the word "minerals" when hereinafter used) which
are now upon or discovered or which shall during the contin-
uance of this demise be discovered within under or upon all
those lands (hereinafter referred to as "the said lands")
situate at and around latitude .... and longitude
.... estimated to contain .... acres more or
less which said lands with the dimensions abuttals and
boundaries thereof are more particularly delineated on the
plan drawn on this deed and thereon edged with a red line.

2.   There are included in this demise and for the purposes
thereof the liberties following:-
     (a) To work and get the minerals and to manufacture and
carry away the same and for that purpose and in connection
therewith to have and exercise in over and upon or under the
said lands all necessary and proper easments rights and
priveleges as contained in this contract necessary and suitable
for this enterprise.
     (b) To open sink dig drive work set up and construct in
upon or under the said lands any pits shafts levels adits
air-holes and to erect set up and afterwards take down and

remove any machinery engines equipment and other plant
houses camps buildings and other erections (for the residence
and accommodations of employees workmen and others employed
in the said mines) and works and to use all such other
means as may be requisite or proper for working and winning
the said minerals to the best advantage and to use all
works of whatever nature now existing on and in connection
with the said lands mines and premises and to wash dress and
render merchantable carry away and dispose of all the said
minerals.

(c) To use any river streams water courses springs or
waters lying or flowing within the said lands or forming
the boundary thereof or any part thereof and to make construct and maintain any water courses culverts drains or
reservoirs for any of the purposes aforesaid but so as not
to prejudice irrigation or deprive any lands houses or
watering places for cattle of a reasonable supply of water
from time to time and not to infringe the rights of any
third party.

(d) To construct and use roads tram roads railways
and all other systems of communications storeage reservoirs
tanks bins and receptacles wharves piers sea loading lines
bins and lighters in connection with the exploration prospecting transportation storeage treatment manufacture or
dealing with exploration of metals or minerals or in connection with the camps buildings and quarters of the personnel
of the Lessees provided always that this shall not extend
to the use of airplanes and wireless within the country which
shall be the subject of a separate agreement or agreements.

It is also understood that the Lessor shall be allowed
to use railway road and port facilities established by the
Lessee so long as such use shall not interfere with the
interests of the Lessee. The form of such use shall be the
subject of a separate agreement between the Lessor and the
Lessee at the time of such need.

(e) To use the said lands or any part thereof for
depositing and heaping thereon the said minerals hereby

demised and all the earth soil and other substances brought to the surface in or about the working of the same.

(f) To search for dig fell cut and use upon and from the said lands all such gravel sand lime stone gypsum and other articles and things as may be required for the making and construction of the houses railways tram roads and other erections and conveniences aforesaid, timber and wood shall be used for domestic purposes only and not for power or construction.

3. The said premises shall be held by the Lessees for the term of fifty eight years commencing from the .... day of .... 19 ...

4. The Lessees during the said term shall pay to the Lessors in respect of the said minerals a yearly rent of one pound sterling for every acre of land hereby demised such rent to be payable in advance on the .... day of .... in each year provided always that if in any one year it shall be found that five per cent of the actual annual value of the minerals produced during that year shall exceed the said sum of one pound sterling per acre then the Lessees shall pay such excess that is to say the sum of which five per cent of such value shall exceed the said sum of one pound sterling per acre by way of further rent or royalty to the Lessors and such excess rent or royalty (if any) shall be payable in each year within three months after the said annual value for such year shall have been ascertained.

All payments under this clause shall be made in such currency and to such bank as the Lessors shall specify at the rates of exchange prevailing at the time of such payment.

As further consideration for the granting of this lease the lessee will if and when they promote a Company or Companies for the purpose of acquiring this lease and the properties comprised herein allot to the Lessors or their

nominee fifteen per cent of the nominal capital of such
Company or Companies in the form of fully paid shares and
the right to appoint one Director on Board of each Company.
Furthermore it is agreed that the number of Directors on
Board of each Company shall be six only of whom one shall
be appointed by the Government and all Directors shall have
equal power. It is understood that such Company or Companies
will be formed when or before commercial production is
reached and the regulations governing such Company shall
have been referred to the Government and it's approval
obtained; such approval shall be deemed granted if no
objection is stated within a period of one month from the
date of the receipt of such notice at Mecca.

5.   The Lessees for themselves and their successors and
assign and to the intent that the obligations may continue
throughout the term hereby created covenant with the Lessors
as follows:-

(a) To pay the reserved rent or royalties on the days and
in manner aforesaid.

(b) Not to conduct work or occupy any religious or sacred
area such as cemeteries mosques etc.

(c) To give the duly authorized representatives of the
Lessors during the usual hours of operation full facilities
and access to all mining operations and records of production of minerals for the purpose of inspecting the work
carried on by the Lessees.

(d) Not to interfere or permit it's employees to interfere
with the administrative political or religious affairs
within Saudi Arabia and in case of any breach of this
provision the person or persons so offending shall at the
instance of the Lessors be liable to deportation from the
said country and after such employee shall have been
punished according to the laws of the country and shall
have been paid the customary indemnity usual for such offence;

Page Five

it being understood that the laws and regulations of Saudi
Arabia shall apply to all employees of the Company in the
same way as they apply to others residing in the country.

(e) That it's operations shall be directed and supervised
by personnel appointed by the Lessees who shall employ Saudi
Arab nationals as far as practicable and will not employ
other nationals as long as Saudi Arabs are competent and
available for such work. It is understood that foreign
subjects of adjacent countries who shall be employed by the
Company - by reason of lack of nationals competent for such
services it shall submit to the Government their names and
identities prior to their definite appointment. If the
Government does not object within a period of one month,
the Company shall consider that the Government has given
it's approval of their employment.

All contracts with Saudi Arab subjects involving a time
exceeding one month shall be submitted to the Government for
it's advice and approval, if the Company does not receive
an adverse reply from the Government within fifteen days
from the time of telegraphing such notice, the approval shall
be deemed as given.

(f) To abide by the existing of future laws of Saudi Arabia
affecting workers in similar industrial enterprises.

(g) To supply the Lessors with copies of all general maps
and reports written in connection with the operations of
the Lessees with reference to the exploration and prospecting
and mining operations carried on in or under the said lands.

(h) To furnish the Lessors for their confidential reference
within six months after the end of each semester a Report of
the operations carried on by the Lessees during the preceeding
semester.

(i) To give the Lessors official agents and personnel on
official business the right to use such communication and

transportation facilities as to the Lessees may establish provided that such use shall not obstruct or interfere with the Lessees operations or impose upon the Lessees any undue burden or expense.

(j) To prosecute the mining operations so as to reach commercial production at the earliest possible date consistent with sound mining practice. Ores are to be treated in Saudi Arabia; precious metals will be reduced to the form of bullion ready for export; and other metals or minerals to the most efficient economic marketable form. It is understood that the Company shall only conduct such treatments if it is economical to do so. Mining operations for the purpose of this sub-clause shall include the ordering and shipping of equipment to Saudi Arabia.

(k) To maintain all landmarks by which boundaries of the said lands are defined and keep all boundary lines open.

(l) To permit the taking and removal without payment from the said lands by any person duly authorized by the Lessors of any earth sand gravel timber or such other road making or building material as shall be approved of by the Lessee and which may be required by the Lessors for any public purpose and are not in use by the Lessee.

(m) To keep or cause to be kept true and sufficient account and records of the mining and other business carried on by the Lessees and of the disposal of metals and minerals obtained from the said lands and will if so required by the Lessors produce or cause to be produced such books and records for the inspection by a duly authorized representative of the Lessors.

(n) The Lessors have the right to pass over the said lands for the purpose of obtaining access to adjoining lands as long as the same shall not interfere with the rights of the Lessees hereby demised under the lease.

(o)   To take all due and proper precautions as may be considered necessary to ensure the health and safety of all miners and workmen employed in connection with the mining operations carried on by the Lessees.

6.   The Lessors hereby covenant with the Lessees as follows:-

(a)   That the Lessees paying the rent or royalties hereby reserved and observing and performing the covenants and provisions on their part herein contained shall peaceably hold and enjoy the promises hereby demised for and during the said term without any interruption by the Lessors or any person rightfully claiming under or any person in trust for them.

(b)   The Lessors shall undertake to protect the Lessees its employees and property. The form of such protection shall be described in detail in special letters which shall be exchanged between the Lessors and Lessees and which shall be subject to modification from time to time as conditions shall vary; it being understood that the Lessees shall pay the Lessors the wages of such guards as shall be agreed.

(c)   To exempt the Lessees and their successors in interest from all direct and indirect taxes import charges fees and export duties on minerals metals and bullion produced but the Lessees shall pay the Lessors Customs Duies of ten per cent of the certified invoice valuation of all its imports. It being understood that such certification shall be made by a Chamber of Commerce, Saudi Arab Legation or in the absence of these by a responsible authority such as Notary Public Court or Government Department. It is further understood that the Lessees shall not sell within the Kingdom any such imported products until the Customs Duties paid by others shall have been paid on such products.

(d)   In times of serious emergency to compensate the Lessees for any use by the Lessors of the Lessees transportation and communication facilities and for any loss which may be sustained by the Lessees thereby whether through damage to the Lessees facilities equipment or operations; it being understood that the Lessors shall not compensate the Lessees for their estimated profits during the period of such emergency use. Furthermore nor shall the Lessors be under obligations to compensate the Lessees for any damage occuring through force majeure.

(e) To cooperate with and render every possible assistance that may be required by the Lessees for the purpose of acquiring from any occupant or owner the surface rights of any land which shall be deemed necessary in connection with the work of prospecting and exploration or mining operations carried on by the Lessees. Provided that the Lessees shall pay to the occupant or owner of such lands for the use thereof such amount as shall be equitable having regard to the customary use made by the occupant or owner of such land plus a reasonable profit.

7.   IT IS HEREBY EXPRESSLY AGREED as follows:-

(a) If the rent hereby reserved or any part thereof shall be in arrear or unpaid for the space of three months next after any of the days or times when the same ought to be paid then and so often as the case shall happen the Lessors will give to the Lessees two months notice requiring payment of the said rent and after the expiration of such notice the Lessors without prejudice to any of the rights of the Lessors for the recovery of the rent or royalties so in arrear enter into and upon the mines and premises thereby demised and may destrain all or any of the metals and minerals engines plant live and dead stock tools implements chattels and things which shall be found in or upon the demised premises and the same may take lead drive carry away and dispose of and out of the monies arising thereby retain and take the rent and royalties which shall then be due and all costs and expenses occassioned by the non-payment thereof and the Lessor shall have the right to cancel the lease.

Page Nine

(b) If the rent or royalties hereby reserved or any part
thereof shall be in arrear or remain unpaid for the space
of six calendar months next after any of the days whereon
the same ought to be paid as aforesaid and not less than
two months notice shall have been given by the Lessors
to the Lessees requiring payment thereof or if the Lessees
shall commit any substantial breach of the covenants and
conditions herein contained and on the part of the Lessees
to be observed and performed and shall fail to remedy such
breach within three calendar months after receiving notice
thereof from the Lessors then and in any such case it shall
be lawful for the Lessors at any time hereafter to enter
into and upon the premises hereby demised or any part thereof in the name of the whole and the same to have again and
repossess and enjoy as of their former estate provided
always that the purposes of this Clause no breach of covenant on the part of the Lessees shall be deemed to have been
committed if such breach shall be occassioned through force
majeure.

8. If at any time during the term hereby demised shall be
destroyed or rendered substantially and permanently unfit
for the purpose of this demise by fire tempest earthquake
or flood of violence of any army or mob or other irresistable
force then these presents shall at the option of the Lessee
be void. Provided that if these presents shall become void
for or by reason of any of the causes aforesaid it shall be
without prejudice to the rights and remedies of the Lessers
for the recovery of any rent or royalties which may have been
committed of any of the covenants herein contained on the
part of the Lessees and which the Lessees may not have
remedied as aforesaid as per item "B" Article 7.

9. If the minerals under the whole or any part of the
said lands shall not at any time be a payable proposition or
if the whole or any part of the said lands shall not be
required by the Lessees then the Lessees shall notwithstand-
ing the term hereby granted be at liberty to surrender the
whole or such part of the said lands as shall not by reason

of the purposes aforesaid by longer required by the Lessees
on giving to the Lessors three calendar months notice in
writing of their intention so to do and thereupon the
Lessees shall pay to the Lessors the rent or royalties
accrued up to the date of such surrender and this demise
and all covenants and conditions herein contained so far
as the same shall relate to the whole or a part of the
lands so surrendered as aforesaid shall forthwith cease and
determine but without prejudice to the rights and remedies
of the Lessors in respect of any antecedent breach of any
of the covenants on the part of the Lessees herein contained.
If a part only of the said lands shall be surrendered the
Lessees shall cause such part to be demarcated and surveyed
and a plan thereof prepared and forwarded to the Lessors at
the time of giving the notice as aforesaid and a copy of
such plan shall be annexed to every copy of this lease and
the original plan annexed thereto shall be deemed to be
amended accordingly.

10.   On the determination of the lease hereby granted the
following provisions shall apply with regard to the assets
of the Lessees:-

(a)   The Lessees immovable property such as roads water wells
permanent buildings structures etc. shall become the property
of the Lessors free of all charges and expenses to the
Lessors and the Lessees shall thereupon be absolved from all
liability in respect thereof.

(b)   The Lessees shall offer their movable property to the
Lessors at a fair price equal to the replacement value of
such property at the time such offer is made less a reasonable sum for the depreciation and if the Lessors shall not
accept said offer within thirty days after the same being
made the Lessees shall then be entitled to remove such
property at any time within a period of six months after
the making of such offer and any property not so removed at
the expiration of that period shall automatically become
the property of the Lessors without any charges.

11. The Lessees after having obtained the approval of the Lessors shall have the right to assign this lease and the benefits thereof shall inure to the benefit of the Lessees its successors or assigns to any company or companies formed for the purpose of acquiring and operating the properties herein contained.

12. All notices required to be given under this lease shall in the case of the Lessors be addressed to the Finance Minister at Mecca and in the case of the Lessees shall be addressed to the authorized representative of the Lessees in Jeddah and all notices shall be sent by prepaid registered post and service thereof shall be deemed to have been affected at the time at which the letter would be delivered in the ordinary course of post.

13. The period of time referred to in this lease shall be calculated on the basis of the solar calendar.

14. It is intended that this lease shall be prepared in Arabic and in English and both texts shall have equal value.

15. If any question dispute or difference shall arise between the Lessors and the Lessees concerning the construction and meaning of these presents or any of the covenants and provisions herein contained or the rights duties and liabilities of either party under or in connection with these presents then in every such case the question dispute or difference shall be referred to two arbitrators one to be appointed by each party and the Referee to be appointed by the Arbitrators. Before proceeding to arbitration each of the parties hereto shall nominate its arbitrator within thirty days of being requested in writing by the other party so to do and in the event of the Arbitrators failing to agree they shall request the President of the Permanent Court of Justice to appoint a Referee. The decision of the Arbitrators or in case of a difference of opinion between them the decision of the Referee shall be final. The Place of arbitration shall be such as may be agreed upon by the

Page Twelve

parties hereto and in default of agreement shall be The Hague Holland.

IN WITNESS whereof the parties hereto have hereunder affixed their respective hands and seals the day and year first above written.

Signed
for and on behalf of the Saudi Arab Government...........

Signed
for and on behalf of the Saudi ....
Arabian Mining Syndicate Limited

Dated 17th. Ramadan 1353
23rd. December 1934

From:-
    Abdullah Suleiman Al Hamdan - Minister of Finance
    to Saudi Arabia

To:- Karl Saben Twitchell - Representative of the Saudi
    Arabian Mining Syndicate Limited.

In accordance with the Mines Concessions Agreement and Exhibit "B" made between you and me on this seventeenth day of Ramadan 1353 (twenty third of December 1934) on behalf of the Saudi Arabian Mining Syndicate Limited and the Saudi Arab Government and whereas the said agreement has defined the exemption of the exports of mineral products from duties I wish to confirm hereby that we have agreed that such exemptions shall not include the sale of mineral products within Saudi Arabia until after the duties which the Government may fix shall have been paid prior to their sale.

146

Your signature hereunder shall indicate your acceptance of the above understanding.

With respects.

Minister of Finance to Saudi Arabia.

....

....

Representative of the Saudi Arabian
Mining Syndicate Limited.

TRADE AGREEMENTS
TA
SEP 4 1935 K

AMERICAN CONSULATE

Aden, Arabia, June 25, 1935.

OFFICE OF ...
AUG 30 1935 R
DEPARTMENT OF STATE

SUBJECT: Mining Concession Granted in Saudi Arabia.

JUL 20 1935

THE HONORABLE

THE SECRETARY OF STATE

WASHINGTON

SIR:

I have the honor to transmit herewith translations, from "Umm el Qura" of Mecca, of the terms of a concession reported to have been granted by the Saudian Government to the Saudi Arabian Mining Syndicate, together with a translation of the notification pertaining thereto. It will be noted that Mr. K. S. Twitchell is named as having acted for the Syndicate in the matter.

There is also enclosed a rough sketch-map, the result of the Consulate's attempt to locate the limits of the concession as they are described in Clause 2 of the translation. Since a number of the places mentioned in Clause 2 could not be found on the Consulate's map, the boundary as shown should be regarded as merely suggestive.

FILED SEP 6 1935

-2-

Information received from Jeddah indicates that the
Syndicate commenced activities in February, 1935.

Respectfully yours,

Leo J. Callanan
American Consul

3 Enclosures:

　　1. Translation of the Notification.

　　2. Translation of the Concession

　　3. Sketch-map

File No. 873/LJC/aob.

Enclosure No. 1. to Despatch No.117 of June 25, 1935.

Translated from Um-el-Qurah of Mecca, February 15, 1935
Notification No. 6091.

<u>Granting a Concession for Mineral Exploration</u>

We, Abdul Aziz Bin Abdul Rehman Al Faisal Al Saud, King
of Saudi Arabia, after perusing the agreement concluded at
Jeddah on December 23, 1934, between our Finance Minister and
Mr. K. S. Twitchell, representative of the Saudi Arabian
Mining Syndicate, Ltd., at London, and after the approval of
the Chamber of Deputies, we have passed the following order:

1. The Saudi Arabian Mining Syndicate Ltd., is to
be permitted to explore for all minerals except oils,
within the territories defined in the agreement attached
to this notification, within our Saudi Kingdom, in
accordance with the stipulations and rules in the agreement
signed by our Finance Minister and the representative of
the said Syndicate at Jeddah on December 23, 1934.

2. We confirm the said agreement, and the two
documents attached to this notification, and order it
to be enforced from the date of publication.

3. Our Finance Minister is to enforce the provisions
of this notification.

Issued from the Riadh Palace on February 12, 1935.

(Signed)   Abdul Aziz

By order of the King
(Signed)   Faisal

150

This agreement was concluded on December 23, 1934, between
Sheikh Abdulla Al-Suleman Al-Hamdan on behalf of the Saudi
Arabian Government (hereinafter called the Government) on the
one hand, and Karol Sabin Twitchell on behalf of the Saudi
Arabian Mining Syndicate, with headquarters at 55-61 Margate,
London, England, on the other hand. The agreement has been
reached between the Syndicate and the Government as follows:

Clause 1

The Government gives to the Syndicate, under the conditions
described below, the right to explore and search on and below
the surface of the earth within the area described in the second
clause, for metals and metallic matters, and for this purpose
the Syndicate may make pits on the surface and underground,
shafts and other excavations. The Government also gives to
the Syndicate all possible facilities as described in this
agreement to enable it to carry out the object mentioned above,
for two years from the date this agreement takes effect or
operates.

Clause 2

The area within which the right of exploration is given
as referred to in this clause, is described in the map attached
to this agreement, and marked (1). Its boundries are:

From longitude 38 degrees east and latitude 29
degrees, 35 minutes North the line extends to the last
boundries of the country under the control of the Saudi
Government at the present time. From Transjordania west
to the Gulf of Akaba and the Red Sea, it extends to the
South as far as the bay of Berak at latitude 18 degrees,
10 minutes North, and the line of boundries extends from
Berak as far as the North-east of the village of Ragdan in
Gamed. Thence it turns to the North-west as far as Berath
Samoodah and continues to the North as far as Ashirah.
From Ashirah to Mohdethah and Kharaba and thence to Merran
and the Akaba, waters within the limits of Kashb. From
the western side it extends from Akaba on a straight line
to Mahd El-Dahab which is about 20 kilometres to the east
of El-Garisiah and thence it extends on a straight line
to the North-west of El-Hanakiah. From El-Hanakiah to the
Hadidiah Station of the Hedjaz Railway leaving Khaiber
outside the limits of the province. Thence it extends

-2-

to the North-west on a straight line to longitude 38
East, and latitude 29 degrees, 35 minutes North and
out of these boundries the suburbs of Medina, not to
exceed 30 kilometres radius, are excluded.

Clause 3

(a) The work of exploration and prospecting in all areas
comprised in the concession will commence within three months
from the date of operation of this agreement, and the Syndicate
is bound to continue the work unless otherwise compelled by
circumstances. The Syndicate must produce within thirty
days from the date of the operation of this agreement the
necessary prospecting equipments.

(b) Not later than a year from the date of the operation
of this agreement the Syndicate is bound to choose the territories in which it desires to search or explore, and the
Syndicate is also required to establish an office at Jeddah
after the expiration of one year from the date of operation
of this agreement.

(c) Not later than two years from the date of operation
of this agreement, the Syndicate will select any places or
territories it desires to take on lease for a period of 58
years from the date on which the lease or leases are granted
for the purpose of carrying out the works of exploration.
This will be done through a company or companies to be formed
by the Syndicate for that purpose.

Clause 4

(a) The Syndicate will not pay to the Government any
rent during the first year as defined in clause 3, under
para (a).

(b) The Syndicate will pay rent to the Government
annually in advance at the rate of four shillings for every
acre (the acre being 4047 Square metres), commencing the

second year, for any land selected by the Syndicate for further exploration as described in clause 3, para (b).

(c) The Syndicate will pay rent to the Government annually in advance at the rate of one pound-sterling for every acre selected by the Syndicate under clause 3, para (c).

(d) The Syndicate will also pay to the Government, during the period of operations, five per cent of the value of the output of metals (before expenses are deducted), or four shillings per acre, whichever is the larger sum.

(e) All payments shall be made to the Bank chosen or approved by the Government, and in the currency desired.

(f) Before the Syndicate can transfer to another company any right for exploring a zone, area or province, it must inform the Government and obtain their approval. The Government, however, will not refuse to comply with the request of the Syndicate unless there are sufficiently important reasons affecting Government interests.

Clause 5

(a) The Government undertake to grant to the Syndicate and its successors any lease or leases in accordance with the form prescribed in schedule (b).

(b) The Government undertake to protect the Syndicate, its employees and possessions. The way in which that protection is to be given shall be detailed in special correspondence to be exchanged between the Government and the Syndicate, and is subject to modification from time to time as required by circumstances, and the Syndicate will pay to the Government all necessary wages for guards or watchmen.

(c) The Government will exempt the Syndicate and its successors from the payment of all taxes and fees on metallic

-4-

metallic matters produced. On imports the Syndicate will pay to the Government ten per cent ad voleram customs duty as shown in invoices which shall be authenticated by responsible quarters, that is to say commercial firms or officials of Saudi Arabia. In the absence of commercial firms or Saudi officials in the place of export, the invoices shall be authenticated by any responsible person such as the clerk of a Court of Justice or other Government department. The Syndicate has no right to sell within the Saudi Arabian Kingdom anything imported by it, on which ten per cent was paid, unless they first pay to the Government full custom duties on the things they wish to sell.

(d) The Government will give to the Syndicate the right to make use of all facilities that may be considered necessary or useful in carrying out the objects of this scheme. These facilities include the construction of roads the erection of tents and buildings, and the improvement of all means of communication.

Also the erection of any machinery or fittings which will be helpful in exploring and searching for these metals or for the transport storage and exportation or experimentation and manufacture of these metals or metallic matters, or anything relating to the erection of tents, buildings or residential quarters or houses for the officials or employees of the Syndicate or companies. Also the construction of harbors and the use of all means for the transport of their officials or articles, gold metallic matters and other products. It is understood, however, that the use of aeroplanes and wireless within this Kingdom will be the subject of a separate agreement between the Government and the Syndicate. The Government have the right to use any railway lines, roads or harbors that may be constructed by the Syndicate without affecting or injuring the

154

interests of the Syndicate. How that is to be done shall form the subject of a separate agreement.

(e) The Government will give to the Syndicate the right to drill and dig for waters and use them, and also make use of any Government waters for the works of the Syndicate, provided this does not affect any irrigation works or destroy any land or houses or cattle.

(f) The Government gives to the Syndicate to make use as within necessary limits, of other products such as earth, stones, lime and other matters resembling them. The Syndicate has the right to use timber and firewood only for household purposes, and not for the erection of any machinery or building.

(g) The Government will compensate the Syndicate for using any means of transport or communication belonging to it at times of emergency, and will pay for any losses that may be suffered by the Syndicate on that account. It is understood however, that the Government is not bound to give any compensation to the Syndicate for the loss of profits that might have been earned by it at such critical times. The Government is not liable for damages or injury suffered by the Syndicate's communications through force of circumstances.

(h) The Government will give to the Syndicate the right to utilize, on the surface, any ground or land that may be considered necessary by the Syndicate for their works of exploration, research and experiments, provided it pays to the owner or occupier an adequate compensation.

Clause 6

The Syndicate is bound to comply with the following stipulations, viz:

(a) Not to undertake or carry out any works within any religious or holy limits or spheres such as cemeteries,

-6-

mosques etc., and not to occupy such places.

(b) The Syndicate shall give to the representatives of
the Government during working hours, all necessary facilities
to enable them to know of its operations and shall keep
registers for examination.

(c) The employees should not interfere with the
administrative, political or religious acts or actions of the
Government within the Saudi Arabian Kingdom, and any officials
contravening this provision will be deported from the country
in addition to other punishment that may be considered
necessary. And it is understood that all the Syndicate's
officials or employees are liable to the same regulations
and laws as other residents within the Saudi Kingdom.

(d) The works of the Syndicate are to be managed and
supervised by persons to be chosen by the Syndicate. These
should be Arabs and Saudi Subjects wherever possible. The
Syndicate must obtain the approval of the Government before
appointing or employing foreign subjects from the adjacent
countries whom the Syndicate may be compelled to employ
owing to the absence of competent persons within the Kingdom.
Also the managers of the Syndicate have no right to enter into
any contracts with Saudi subjects for works extending over
one month unless they obtain the sanction of the Government.

(e) The Syndicate shall submit to the laws and regulations of the Saudi Arabian Government which are now in
force or that may be enforced in the future within the Kingdom.

(f) The Syndicate shall submit to the Government copies
of maps and plans that may be prepared in connection with the
works to be carried out by the Syndicate.

(g) The Syndicate shall submit every six months, to the

-7-

Government a list of its works for the information of the Government.

(h) The Syndicate will permit the Government officials or their representatives to use the means of transport and communication belonging to the Syndicate, provided this will not hamper or handicap the Syndicate's works in accordance with this agreement.

(i) In accordance with this agreement when the Government grants any lease to the Syndicate under clause 5, para (a), as explained above, and as soon as the Syndicate, from the data available, is prepared to start work, it will form a company or companies, on its own account, to work the mines with the necessary equipment for extracting metallic matters. The Syndicate will pay to the Government a sum equal to fifteen per cent of the capital of the company or companies in return for the lease thus granted, and the company or companies are bound to submit to the conditions of the lease as detailed in (b). At the same time it will offer to Saudi Arabian subjects ten per cent of the shares of the company or companies to be offered for sale to the public, to be accepted or rejected in the course of thirty days.

The Syndicate is also bound to carry out the works expeditiously and diligently as soon as possible according to mining principles.

(j) The said lease or leases provide that the company or companies which will be formed shall pay to the Government five per cent of the value of the output from the date of the grant of the lease or leases.

Clause 7

(a) This agreement will be annulled or rescinded by the Government if the Syndicate, except for sufficient cause, stops all works in the Saudi Arabian country for a period exceeding three months and in that case the

8

Government will give notice to the Syndicate either by
letter or by telegraph annulling the concession. The
Syndicate will be considered as having stopped their works
if it has no competent representative in the Saudi Arabian
Kingdom for three successive months.

(b) The Syndicate will have the right to stop the
works in any areas where investigations are carried on,
upon giving notice by letter or telegram, to the Government,
thirty days before stopping the works.

No works should be stopped under any circumstances
for more than three months, except for sufficient causes.
In that case the Government have the right under para (a)
to rescind the concession.

(c) When the agreement is thus rescinded by such a notice,
or for any other reason or reasons, the Syndicate shall be
free from all obligations under the agreement, except the
following:

(1) The possessions or belongings of the Syndicate,
such as roads, waters, wells and immoveable railways
and machines etc., shall pass to the Government without
any return.

(2) The Syndicate shall offer to the Government their
moveable belongings in Saudi Arabia at moderate rates.
If the Government refuses to accept them within 30 days
after rescinding the agreement, the Syndicate must remove
them in six months. If these belongings or things or
parts of them, are not removed in this period they will
become the property of the Government without any return
or compensation.

Clause 8

(a) The Regulations and Rules shall not conflict with

the Regulations and Rules of the Kingdom.

(b) The solar calender is the approved calender in this agreement.

(c) This agreement was drawn up in Arabic and English and shall be considered as one.

(d) Any short-coming or negligence by the Syndicate in ovserving any condition in this agreement will not be considered by the Government as contravening or infringing the agreement if the negligence or failure was caused by unforseen circumstances.

(e) In the case of any difference during the operation of the agreement, about its interpretation or execution, or relating to any rights or obligations, concerning which agreement can not be reached, the differences shall be referred to two arbitrators, each party to appoint one arbitrator and an umpire to be chosen by the two arbitrators. Each party shall appoint his arbitrator within thirty days from the date of receipt of notification. If the two arbitrators differ as regards the umpire, the Government and Syndicate will agree to appoint him; and if they do not agree about the arbitrators, the president of the Court of Justice will be asked to choose them. The arbitrators' decision shall be final, and if they differ the decision of the umpire shall be final. The place of arbitration shall be selected by both parties, and if they fail to agree it shall be the Hague, Holland.

(f) This agreement after being signed in Saudi Arabia shall be sent by the Syndicate to its office in London, England, for ratification. It shall not be operative unless thus ratified by the Syndicate. If the Syndicate does not ratify it within 10 days from the date of receipt of the agreement, it will become null and void, and of no effect.

-10-

If the Syndicate ratifies this agreement, it shall send back to the Government one copy of each text, with the necessary endorsement confirming its ratification. Thereafter the Government will publish it in the usual way in Saudi Arabia.

(g) As regards notices to be issued under this agreement, those for the Government, shall be addressed to the Finance Minister at Mecca, and those for the Syndicate, to the agent of the Syndicate at Jeddah.

(h) The Syndicate has the right, after obtaining the approval of the Government to transfer any rights granted under this agreement to any special company or companies that may be formed for working and exploring the mines.

Signed by Abdulla Al-Suleman Al-Hamdan on behalf of the Government, and Karol Sabin Twitchell on behalf of the Syndicate, on the day, month and year mentioned above.

160

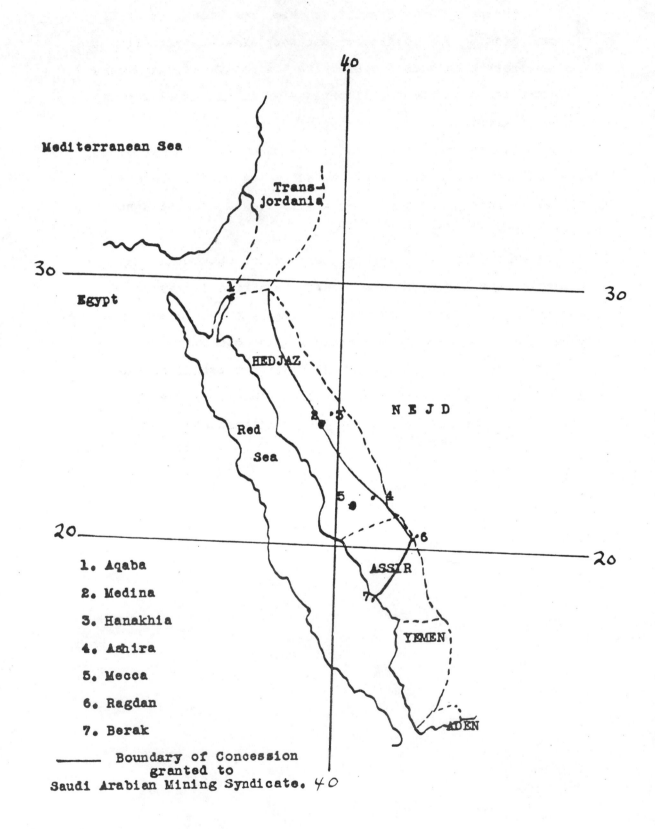

Mediterranean Sea

Trans-
jordania

Egypt

HEDJAZ

N E J D

Red

Sea

ASSIR

YEMEN

ADEN

1. Aqaba

2. Medina

3. Hanakhia

4. Ashira

5. Mecca

6. Ragdan

7. Berak

————— Boundary of Concession
granted to
Saudi Arabian Mining Syndicate.

890f.6363

DOCUMENT FILE

NOTE

SEE 890g.00 General conditions/62 ___ FOR ___ #528 ___

FROM ___ Iraq ___ (Slavens) DATED Sept.18, 1935
TO   NAME   1—1127   •••

REGARDING:
Report that large oil deposits exist in Hassa.

890F.6363/15   / S

Wi

OIL FLOW IN HASSA.

A report from Basrah is that individuals arriving
from the Persian Gulf state that laborers in Hassa digging
up mud encountered a flow of oil which spread to neighboring
plains and valleys and passed through irrigation ditches
like water. The report adds that this occurrence has
had a strong effect in political and economic circles
in the Gulf and in Saudi Arabia.[2]

> Comment: This sounds too good to be true. The
> Charge d'Affaires of Saudi Arabia has
> informed this Legation that he knows
> nothing of the matter aside from the
> news item.

SAUDI ARABIAN MINING SYNDICATE, LIMITED.

DIRECTORS
LOUIS HARDY.
Alternate G. H. HUTTON (U.S.A.)
H. R. EDWARDS (U.S.A.)
E. D. McDERMOTT.

MANAGER
K. S. TWITCHELL.

Jiddah,

Hejaz,

Saudi Arabia.

November 22, 1935.

Wallace Murray, Esq.,
Chief, Division of Near Eastern Affairs,
Department of State,
Washington, D.C.

Dear Mr. Murray;

Your letter of September 19 reached me after I returned from a hurried trip to London and New York. The next time I return to U.S.A. I hope I may have the pleasure of seeing you in Washington.

Yes, you are correct in understanding that American interests - The American Smelting & Refining Company - now control the management of this Syndicate; that was the understanding when they bought their interest.

// At present I have 21 on my staff of whom four are Americans, shortly there will/be probably two to four more American engineers and two aviators. Besides these men in Hijaz there are 17n Americans in El Hassa, Saudi Arabia connected with the Standard Oil of California; if the contemplated second well is drilled in Hassa there will be five to ten more Americans. There are two Americans permanently in Jiddah representing the Oil Company. So you see there is developing quite a colony.

I shall be glad when I can go to an American

SAUDI ARABIAN MINING SYNDICATE, LIMITED.

DIRECTORS
LOUIS HARDY.
Alternate G. H. HUTTON (U S A
H. R. EDWARDS (U.S.A.)
E. D. McDERMOTT.

MANAGER
K. S. TWITCHELL

IN REPLY PLEASE QUOTE
....

Jiddah,

Hejaz,

Saudi Arabia.

7 U. 11 9 0 F

Legation to have documents legalized instead of to the
British or the Dutch as is now necessary. We have
six Swedish diamond drillers at work at the mines and
they are minus diplomatic representation the same as
the Americans.

The Italians have a Legation and so have
the French; the commercial interests of both are practically
nil; nor have they the Moslem subjects like the Dutch.
The Italians are trying hard to secure various contracts
and concessions but so far they are unsuccessful.   It is
a rather interesting fact that all other nations establish
diplomatic representatives to assist their nationals
abroad. Do you not agree ? //

Kindest regards and best wishes for
Christmas and the New Year.

Yours sincerely,

K.S.Twitchell

DEPARTMENT OF STATE

Memorandum of Conversation

DATE: December 10, 1937.

SUBJECT: Activities of the Iraq Petroleum Company.

PARTICIPANTS: Mr. Harold Greene of the Export Department of the Socony-Vacuum Oil Corporation;

Mr. P. H. Alling.

COPIES TO:
Baghdad
Beirut
Jerusalem

During a recent call which Mr. Greene made at the Department in connection with another matter I asked him about the operations of the Iraq Petroleum Company, particularly about development of the former British Oil Development Concession in northwestern Iraq. Mr. Greene stated that, as we probably knew, the crude oil found in that concession area was a particularly heavy type and that the company's technical experts were inclined to believe that it could not be pumped through the existing IPC pipeline without injury to the better grade of crude found in the IPC development to the east of the Tigris River. Consideration was therefore being given to the construction of another pipeline to carry to the Mediterranean the crude oil produced

in the former B. O. D. Co. concession. If such a line
were constructed it would probably have its outlet at
Latakia. Consideration was also being given to the feasi-
bility of transporting the crude oil from the former
B. O. D. concession area by tank car over the old Baghdad
railway to Alexandretta. If that plan were adopted it
would, of course, be necessary to extend the railway from
the Syrian-Iraq frontier (its present terminus) to the
oil fields in Iraq.

I asked Mr. Greene if the concessions obtained in
Syria and Saudi Arabia by the companies interested in the
IPC were actually held in the name of the IPC. He replied
that the companies holding such concessions were separate
organizations such as Petroleum Concessions, Ltd. (Syria)
and Petroleum Concessions, Ltd. (Saudi Arabia) but that
the various companies constituting the IPC held interests
in those organizations in the same proportion to their
interests in the IPC. He said the reason for this was
that under the IPC concession in Iraq the Iraqi Government
had an official sitting in the board of directors of the
IPC. Obviously there was no valid reason why the Iraqi
Government should have a representative on the board of
the company when decisions were being taken regarding
concessions in other countries. Hence it was considered

-3-

necessary to form these separate companies to handle

affairs in countries other than Iraq.

NE PHA/HO

Ans'd 8/3/38
NE-890C/SC.

Department of State
Near Eastern Affairs

Gentlemen:

890F.6363   During the past 27 years
I have made various journeys
into Arabia from Syria, Trans-
Jordan, Iraq & the Persian Gulf
covering Central, Eastern &
Western Arabia in many
sections.

The American Geographical
Society in N.Y. (156 & Broadway)
published my map on
the migration-lines of the
Bedouin-tribes, Little, Brown
in Boston published my book
& in various other countries
(England, France, etc.) I have
also published books & articles on Arabia & other parts
of the Near East.

②

I am interested to know what mineral & oil-concessions King Ibn Saud of Saudi Arabia has granted to various American & Foreign Companies & how these boundaries of the concessions are distributed.

While in Arabia I have come across minerals (manganese) and oil prospects, though I am not a geologist,

I want to check on my own map & compare with the maps of the concessions granted to the Shell, Standard oil, etc. etc. where my prospects are located.

Where could I get such information, maps, etc.~ (if not from you). or if you have such maps, could I pay for

170

copies (photostatic or otherwise ③).

I cannot get (I have tried) correct + complete information from oil-companies here + abroad.

I am specially interested to know who has the <u>oil-concessions</u> for NEJD and QASIM . I understand that concessions in HASSA belongs to the Standard-Oil . I am also interested to know who has the mineral (manganese) rights in HEJAZ .

(over, please

(F)

I wish to thank you in
advance for any information
you might be able to
give to me.

very gratefully yours,

Carl N Dalwaan.

CARL R. RASWAN
6939 TRENOR - ST.
OAKLAND.
California.

[3 f stamp included]

July 26/1938.

172

August **4 1938.**

In reply refer to
NE

810 F. 6363

My dear Mr. Raswan:

I have received your letter of July 26, 1938 requesting
to be informed of the mineral and oil concessions granted by
His Majesty Abdul Aziz ibn Saud, King of Saudi Arabia, to
American and foreign companies, including the boundaries of
such concessions, with a reference to any maps which may
have been published on the subject.

In the July 1938 issue of <u>World Petroleum</u>, published
by Mr. Russell Palmer, of 95 River Street, Hoboken, New
Jersey, you will find an oil map of the Near and Middle
East, which includes the areas of the two oil concessions
granted by the Saudi Arabian Government to the California-
Arabian Standard Oil Company and to the Petroleum Development (Western Arabia) Limited, respectively. In the same
publication will be found an article on the activities of
the California-Arabian Standard Oil Company, while brief
notices concerning the companies mentioned above are contained in the Oil and Petroleum Year Book compiled annually

Mr. Carl R. Raswan,
6939 Trenor Street,
Oakland, California.

-2-

by Mr. Walter E. Skinner, 15 Dowgate Hill, London E. C. 4, England.

The only other concession in Saudi Arabia with an American participation known to the Department is one for the exploitation of mineral resources other than oil granted on February 15, 1935, according to the terms of the concession published in Umm el Qura of Mecca on that date, to Mr. K. S. Twitchell, an American citizen, acting on behalf of the Saudi Arabian Mining Syndicate, Limited, with offices at 55 Margate, London, England. It is understood that the original area involved an extent of some 120,000 square miles along the Red Sea Coast of Saudi Arabia, exclusive of certain areas in the vicinity of Mecca and Medina.

For more precise details of the concessions named, other than such information as may be available concerning the oil concessions in the publications mentioned above, it is suggested that you may wish to consider communicating with the companies concerned. The offices of the Petroleum Development (Western Arabia) Limited, are listed as City Gate House, Finsbury Square, London E. C. 2, England. The California-Arabian Standard Oil Company may be reached in care of the Standard Oil Company of California, Standard Oil Building, San Francisco, California, while the address of the Saudi Arabian Mining Syndicate, Limited, is given

-5-

above.

The Department has no information concerning oil and mining concessions granted in Saudi Arabia other than those mentioned.

Sincerely yours,

For the Secretary of State:

Wallace Murray,
Chief, Division of Near Eastern Affairs

AUG 4 1938. CR

NE JRC/GC&EG

A true copy of the signed original.

DOCUMENT FILE

NOTE

SEE _____ 890g.00 General Conditions/145 FOR _____ #1240 _____ _____

FROM __ Iraq _____ _____ (__ Knabenshue __) DATED _____ Feb.17,1939 ___
TO   NAME   1—1127   •••

REGARDING: German oil concessions in Saudi Arabia.
            Press comments concerning the seeking of -- by Dr.Grobba,
            German Minister at Baghdad.

lec

6. <u>GERMAN OIL CONCESSIONS IN SAUDI ARABIA</u>

Dr. Grobba, the German Minister at Baghdad, has left for Jeddah. We now understand that he has visited the senior officials of the Government, that he has asked His Majesty King Ibn Saud to grant Germany a concession to exploit oil along the seashore near the area within the concession of the American company, and that his

request

- 5 -

request is now under consideration.

                    --Al-Difa' Al-Qawmi, February 1, 1939.

Comment: The departure of Dr. Grobba for Jeddah
            on January 17 was reported in my Cur-
            rent Events despatch of February 2nd.
            He has not yet returned. The above
            report is from the first issue of the
            new organ of the Palestine Defense
            Society. The German Chargé d'Affaires
            here has remarked informally that the
            reports that Dr. Grobba is seeking oil
            and gold concessions in Saudi Arabia
            are absurd.

Despatch No. 102, April 22, 1943 from J. Harold Shullaw, American Charge
d'affaires ad interim, Jidda, on the subject: Shaikh Yusuf Yassin and the
California Arabian Standard Oil Company

MEMORANDUM OF CONVERSATION

April 19, 1943

STRICTLY CONFIDENTIAL

Subject: Shaikh Yusuf Yassin and the California Arabian
Standard Oil Company.

Participants: Shaikh Yusuf Yassin, Advisor of King Ibn
Saud.
Mr. Shullaw.

Returning from Riyadh to Jidda Shaikh Yusuf Yassin
and I had stopped for coffee at one of the fuel depots.
In the course of a conversation about the plant of the
California Company at Dhahran, Shaikh Yusuf suddenly
remarked that the oil company was very "tight fisted" and
"hard" in its relations with the Government. Saudi Arabia,
he said, was in a very difficult financial position because
of the war and yet the oil company had done nothing to help.
At this point I ventured the remark that it was my understanding that the oil company had advanced the Saudi
Government considerable sums of money. To this Shaikh
Yusuf replied that the company had "helped a little" but
that their help was very small in comparison with what they
might do since they were so extremely wealthy. He stated
that the oil company could easily fill the small room in
which we were sitting with gold sovereigns and that in any
case the wealth of the oil fields was such that the company
could easily advance larger sums against a certain return
from their investment in future years. My reply to this
was that these were difficult times for oil companies as
well as governments and I further referred to the fact that
the company had certain responsibilities to its stock
holders which controlled its actions. From his comments
at this point it was apparent that Shaikh Yusuf had little
conception of the organization or workings of a large
corporation.

Shaikh Yusuf then referred to the terms of the California
Company's concession and compared it unfavorably with the
concession held by the Iraqi Petroleum Company. In this
connection he made two points: 1) The Iraqi concession
guaranteed the Iraqi Government a minimum annual royalty.
Saudi Arabia under its concession drew its royalties only on
actual production. 2) The Iraqi Government received 20%
of the production of the wells while Saudi Arabia received
from the California Company only a "small amount" of gasoline
and kerosene each year.

Shaikh Yusuf's closing remark was to the effect that
"after the war your Government must help us against the
Company." At this point his conversation was interrupted
by the arrival of our car and I made no reply to his remark.
The conversation on this subject was not resumed.

No. 102

LEGATION OF THE
UNITED STATES OF AMERICA

Jidda, Saudi Arabia, April 22, 1943

STRICTLY CONFIDENTIAL

Subject: Shaikh Yusuf Yassin and the California
Arabian Standard Oil Company

The Honorable
The Secretary of State,
Washington.

Sir:

I have the honor to report that during my recent trip
to Riyadh I traveled with Shaikh Yusuf YASSIN who was the
subject of this Legation's despatch no. 49 dated September
20, 1942. Shaikh Yusuf proved to be extraordinarily
communicative and on one occasion in the course of the
journey spoke at some length on the subject of Saudi Arabian
relations with the California Arabian Standard Oil Company.
It should be pointed out, however, that his remarks must be
taken as a reflection of his own attitude toward the company
and should not necessarily be regarded as the opinion of
King IBN SAUD or of the Minister of Finance, Abdullah
SULEIMAN. A memorandum of the conversation on the subject
is submitted as an enclosure to this despatch.

There is no question of Yusuf Yassin's hostility to
the oil company nor of his willingness to cause any
embarrassment possible in relations between the Saudi Government and the company. His attitude apparently is compounded
of avarice and ignorance. Personal aggrandizement has
characterized his stay in Saudi Arabia and he is not adverse
to aiding his personal position by gaining financial concessions to Saudi Arabia from the company. Ignorance of the
organization of a large corporation and of the nature of its
resources causes him to ignore all practical considerations
of what the oil company might be expected to do for Saudi
Arabia. The simplicity of his approach is best summed up in
his statement that the company is very wealthy, so wealthy
that it can fill a large room with gold sovereigns.

At the present time Abdullah Suleiman, Minister of
Finance, is the chief advisor of Ibn Saud and Shaikh Yusuf
is second in importance among the advisors. Enmity exists
between the two men and Shaikh Yusuf as an intriguer has a
certain advantage over the Minister of Finance who has a
concrete program for the betterment of conditions in Saudi
Arabia. Abdullah Suleiman, in fact, is one of the few
advisors of the King who is sincerely interested in the
progress of the country. Since Abdullah Suleiman has set
out to develop agriculture in the kharj district and in
pursuance of his plans has spent considerable sums of money,
he has laid himself open to attacks from individuals such as
Yusuf Yassin if he does not succeed in his ventures. Shaikh
Yusuf while holding a secondary importance in the councils
of the Kingdom does, nevertheless, possess considerable power

- 2 -

for evil so far as the relations of the company with the
Government are concerned since through his easy access
to the King he is in a position to plant seeds of discord
and nourish misunderstandings. Furthermore, in the event
of a fall from favor of Abdullah Suleiman or of the
Minister's death, Shaikh Yusuf is in a good position to
become first advisor of the King.

For these reasons his hostility to the company is of
considerable importance, both at present and in the
future.

Respectfully yours,

J. Harold Shullaw
Chargé d'affaires ad interim

To Department in triplicate.

Copy to the American Legation at Cairo.

863.6

JHS/cjm

WAR DEPARTMENT
WASHINGTON

The Honorable,
1944 OCT 2 PM 1 21
The Secretary of State.

Dear Mr. Secretary:

A situation has arisen at Bahrein, an island in the Persian Gulf ruled by an Arab sheik, and at Ras Tanurah, on the mainland in the kingdom of Saudi Arabia near-by, which is causing serious concern to this department. At each place oil wells and a refinery are being developed by American interests, whose product is necessary for military use by the United Nations.

At each place there are nearly a thousand American workmen now employed, whose numbers will be later much increased. In such a community an effective and appropriate system of criminal justice is indispensable; but at present the only law to which these men are amenable is the primitive and unsuitable Mohammedan law, enforced by Sikh police. A recent incident at Bahrein demonstrated the serious, almost inevitable, danger of friction when native police seek to arrest Americans.

The proposal has been informally made that the British political agent at Bahrein appoint Americans as peace officers with authority to arrest fellow Americans; and that the agent, with American "assessors" appointed by himself, sit as judge for the trial of Americans there. The War Department approves of that proposal and recommends that it be put into operation as soon as practicable.

A suitable solution for the problem in Saudi Arabia would appear to be the appointment by the king of an American as a special judge to administer a code of laws promulgated by the king and suitable for Americans. This special jurisdiction would extend only to the limited area occupied by Americans, which fortunately is remote and isolated from any Arab centers. The judge would be given authority to appoint Americans as peace officers with power to arrest Americans, thus minimizing friction with native police. From information that the War Department has received it believes that the proposal above outlined would be acceptable to the king.

Because of the dangerous consequences to be expected if an adequate method of enforcing law and order is not soon instituted, and because of the importance of the efficient operation of this refinery to the war effort, I strongly recommend that action looking to some suitable solution be taken promptly.

Sincerely yours,

Henry L. Stimson
Secretary of War.

ARABIAN AMERICAN OIL COMPANY

SAN FRANCISCO, CALIFORNIA

October 9, 1944

ADDRESS REPLY TO
SHOREHAM BUILDING
WASHINGTON, D. C.

Mr. C. B. Rayner, Petroleum Advisor
Department of State
Washington, D. C.

Dear Mr. Rayner:

During recent months the American Army Air Forces
carried out rather extensive aerial photographic surveys in
Saudi Arabia. In large part these aerial surveys have
covered areas which are embraced within our concessions in
Saudi Arabia and you can readily appreciate the valuable
assistance which these photographs would be to us, both in
respect to our geological and exploration program and our
general operations in the country.

Our people in Cairo discussed with USAFIME headquarters the question of obtaining prints of these photographs and we are advised they are entirely agreeable to our
being supplied with copies of these prints and I understand
have referred the matter to Washington. It was suggested to
us here that we initiate our request for copies of these
prints through Army-Navy Petroleum Board. Accordingly, we
addressed such a request to Army-Navy Petroleum Board, attention Major E. P. Kavanaugh. I was under the impression that
your office had had some correspondence with the War Department concerning the release of these pictures to us. I understand now, however, that this correspondence related to
pictures in Egypt and did not specifically cover Arabia.
It has been suggested that it would be helpful if your office
would advise the War Department that the State Department
approves the release of these photographs to us.

As indicated above, we are following the matter with
Major Kavanaugh but any way in which the Department may be
able to facilitate the release of these photographs to Army-
Navy Petroleum Board for us will be greatly appreciated.

Yours very truly,

ARABIAN AMERICAN OIL COMPANY

Garry Owen

GO:PT

In reply refer to
FC/L

Date: October 20, 1944

CONFIDENTIAL J.E.B.

MEMORANDUM

TO: Lieutenant Colonel Edward H. Miller,
Liaison Officer with the Department of State,
Military Intelligence Division,
War Department.

FROM: Liaison Officer

SUBJECT: Release of Arabian photography to Arabian
American Oil Company.

With reference to my memorandum to you of August 29,
1944 on the subject of the release of Egyptian photography to a foreign oil company, I am now in receipt
of a self-explanatory memorandum dated October 16, 1944
from Mr. James C. Sappington, Assistant Chief of the
Petroleum Division of the Department of State.

It will be appreciated if you will bring the
substance of the attached memorandum to the attention
of Major E. P. Kavanaugh of the Army-Navy Petroleum
Board.

Robert Dudley Longyear
Acting Assistant Chief, Division of
Foreign Activity Correlation
Liaison, War-Navy

Enclosure:

As stated above.

FC/L:RDL:JEB

JEB

DEPARTMENT OF STATE

~~OFFICE OF THE PETROLEUM ADVISER~~

PETROLEUM DIVISION

October 16, 1944

FC/L - Mr. Longyear:

Sometime ago a request of the War Department for
an expression of State Department policy for a release
of aerial mapping photography covering northern Egypt
was referred to PED by FC/L. The expression of policy
formulated in my memorandum of August 14, 1944 referred
only to northern Egypt because that was the only area
mentioned in the request.

It now appears that the Arabian American Oil Company is very anxious to secure similar photography of
Saudi Arabia, and the Washington representative of
that company approached the War Department directly
on the assumption that the State Department's policy
expression had been generalized. The War Department
is unwilling to release the Arabian photography unless
written approval is secured from the State Department.
There obviously could be no objection on policy grounds
to the release of the Arabian photography in question,
since the Arabian American Oil Company is the sole concessionnaire in Saudi Arabia and no competitive disadvan-
tages could possibly accrue to other companies. Therefore, unless there are strategic considerations on the
part of the War Department, the Department of State
would favor the release of the photography on whatever
terms seem reasonable to the War Department and the
company. I should appreciate it if you would so inform
the War Department, attention Major E. P. Kavanaugh of
the Army-Navy Petroleum Board.

James C. Sappington
Assistant Chief

PED:JAL:AW

September 2, 1944

M E M O R A N D U M

Re: Possible Assignment of a Police
Instructor to Saudi, Arabia

        On August 31, 1944, Mr. Garry Owen, Washington, D. C., representative
of the California Arabian Oil Company, discussed the matter of assignment of
a Bureau police instructor in a liaison capacity with the Arabian Government.
Mr. Owen stated that he had discussed this matter with Colonel Eddy, new Minister
to Arabia, prior to the latter's departure for his post last week. Colonel Eddy
is planning to discuss the question with King Ibn Saud, and if the Government
is receptive, he will communicate with the State Department concerning the
matter.

        Mr. Owen further advised that the original request of the Arabian
Government had been for the California Arabian Oil Company to conduct the school
through one of its employees. This, however, is not in line with the policy
of the Company, and the question will probably be left to the State Department
for decision. It appears that the State Department and the Company have also
considered the possibility of using Colonel Schwartzkopf, who is presently
engaged in police work in the Near East to take over the instructing job in
Arabia.

        Mr. Owen advised that he was planning to have a further informal
conversation with the State Department in the near future at which time he
will suggest that no problems would arise if a Bureau Agent were assigned to
handle the police instruction work.

PETROLEUM DIVISION

MAY 3 1 1949

DEPARTMENT OF STATE

THE FOREIGN SERVICE
OF THE
UNITED STATES OF AMERICA

AMERICAN EMBASSY

Action Assigned to ....
RESTRICTED
Action Taken ....

Cairo, Egypt,   May 19, 1949

Date of Action 6/1/49

Action Office Symbol ITI

Name of Officer ....

No. 497.   Direction to DC/R ....

890r.6363/5-1949

Subject: Summary of Petroleum Concessions Limited
              1936 contract in the Hedjaz.

        The officer in charge of the American Embassy at
Cairo has the honor to enclose herewith a copy of a summary of the Petroleum Concessions Limited 1936 contract
in the Hedjaz. It is believed that the Department does
not have a copy of this lapsed concession contract.

        Aramco's Jidda representative, Garry Owen, stated
that the concessions of IPC subsidiaries in the Arab
Sheikdoms of Qatar, Muscat, Oman, Aden, which are also
believed to be absent from the Department files, closely
follow the pattern of this contract.

OFFICE OF
INTERNATIONAL TRADE POLICY

MAY 3 1 1949

DEPARTMENT OF STATE

Summary of Petroleum Concessions
Limited 1936 contract in the Hedjaz.

Copies to: NEA, PED
File No. 523.1
RFunkhouser/mw

186

Page 1 of Enclosure No. 1 to Cairo Desptach 497 dated May 19, 1948.

C-o-p-y

SUMMARY OF CONTRACT BETWEEN SAUDI ARAB GOVERNMENT
AND PETROLEUM CONCESSIONS LIMITED - WESTERN SAUDI ARABIA

Date of Contract:	July 9, 1936.
Term:	Sixty years
Area Covered:	The whole of the western coastal region of Saudi Arabia, beginning at the Trans-Jordan boundary and stretching to the south, with a width of 100 kilometers, to the Yemen border. Includes territorial water and islands.
Definition of Commercial Quantities:	A production of not less than 2,000 tons of oil daily for 30 days from one well, or from a number of wells situated within a circle of 25 kilometers diameter; provided that if regular export should commence from any part of the Concession Area, whether from a daily production of 2,000 tons or less, such production shall be considered as commercial quantities.
Subsidiary Company:	Company may transfer its rights, obligations and privileges to a subsidiary company which shall have the same nationality as the original company. The company, or the parent company, shall open an office in Jeddah.
Restriction Against Assignment:	Neither the parent nor subsidiary company is permitted without written consent of the Government to transfer agreement to any person or company, under penalty of forefeiture.
Price of Concession:	30,000 English gold sovereigns ($252,000 U.S. Cy. +). No part of this amount shall be recoverable.
Exploration Period:	Four years for geological investigations and other field work. Company to decide between the sixth and ninth month of the last year whether

RESTRICTED

it intends to drill or not. If Company decides
not to drill, contract terminates. May be extended for fifth year upon sufficient showing
of need for further time to complete exploration
work.

Annual Rental
during Explor-
ation Period:

7,500 English gold sovereigns.
($63,000 U.S. Cy. +).

Drilling
Obligations:

After exploration period, or if earlier decision is made to drill, the Company shall begin
drilling as follows:

First Year: Drill with two rigs, and pay
annual rental of 7,500 gold
sovereigns ($63,000 U.S. Cy. +);

Second Year: Drill with two rigs, and pay
annual rental of 7,500 gold
sovereigns ($63,000 U.S. Cy. +);

Third Year: Drill with two rigs, and pay
annual rental of 10,000 gold
sovereigns ($84,000 U.S. Cy. +);
or with three rigs and pay annual
rental of 7,600 English gold
sovereigns ($63,000 U.S. Cy. +);

Fourth Year: Drill with two rigs and pay annual
rental of 10,000 gold sovereigns
($84,000 U.S. Cy. +); or with three
rigs and pay 7,500 gold sovereigns
($63,000 U.S. Cy. +) as rental;

Fifth Year: Drill with at least three rigs and
pay 10,000 gold sovereigns ($84,000
U.S. Cy. +) as rental;

Second
Five-Year
Period:

Drill with at least three rigs and
pay annual rental of 10,000 gold
pounds ($84,000 U.S. Cy. +).

If oil is not discovered in commercial quantities during first ten
years of drilling, either an agreement shall be made for a further period upon new conditions, or failing agreement, the Government may cancel
contract. If after cancellation, another company applies for concession,
Government shall give preference to original Concessionnaire Company
as against any other, if conditions offered by each are equivalent.

188

Rental After Discovery:	After discovery of oil in commercial quantities, pay annual rental of 10,000 gold sovereigns until regular export commenced, which shall not be postponed for more than two years from date of discovery in commercial quantities.
Relinquishments:	Company to relinquish at least 2/3 of total area within three years after decision made to drill. Within five years thereafter, if oil not found in commerical quantities, Company to relinquish at least half of remaining areas. At end of a further ten years, if oil in commercial quantities not yet discovered, Company to relinquish all remaining area and concession be cancelled.
Royalty to Government:	4 shillings gold for each ton produced, at well head after subtracting therefrom:

(1) Water and foreign substance.
(2) All amounts used in operations within the Concession Area.
(3) All quantities offered free to Government under provisions of agreement.

Natural Gas: If natural gas produced and sold, royalty to be 1/8 of produce of such sale.

Loans:	Upon discovery of oil in commercial quantities, Company to loan Government 50,000 gold sovereigns ($420,000 U.S. Cy. +) and further loan of 50,000 gold sovereigns one year thereafter (if regular export has not yet begun). Recoverable from difference between royalty due on production and Minimum Royalty.
Guaranteed Minimum Royalty:	Company to commence regular export within two years from date of commercial discovery; and beginning at date of regular export Company shall pay a Minimum Royalty of 150,000 gold sovereigns ($1,200,000 U.S. Cy. +), per year. If tonnage royalty due in any one year is less than the Minimum Royalty, Company shall pay Minimum Royalty in full and recover difference from amounts of royalty in future years in excess of Minimum Royalty.
Free Oil:	Company shall give Government 1% of well-head production, which Government may use for public works and other activities. After three years after commercial discovery, Company to give Government annually 300,000 English gallons of gasoline and 200,000 English gallons of kerosene.

Labor Restrictions:	Company to employ Saudi Arab subjects except for technical and administrative officials and other personnel whose duties no subject of Saudi Arabia can be found able to perform. Company to offer all reasonable facilities to train and teach laborers, to improve them and raise their position in the Company.
Maps & Reports:	Company to give Goverment copies of all maps and drawings and all information it may obtain during the exploration, drilling or exploitation periods; to be treated as confidential by Government. Company to submit to Government at end of third month of each year a report in Arabic, dealing with all the Company's operations in the previous year.
Tax Exemptions:	Company and enterprise exempt from all direct and indirect taxes, imposts, charges, fees and duties, except as to products sold within the country and personal requirements of individual employees, and such municipal taxes as are collected from all alike.
Termination:	Company may terminate agreement at any time, upon three months' notice. Government may terminate agreement or take over property of the Company in the Concession Area in the following cases: (1) If Company should fail to make any required payment within six months of due date; (2) If Company defaults under an Arbitration Award.
Arbitration:	All disputes under contract are to be submitted to arbitration, if not otherwise settled. One arbitrator to be chosen by each party, and if the two arbitrators, or the Government and the Company, fail to agree upon the referee, they shall request the President of the Permanent Court of International Justice to appoint the referee. The decision of the two arbitrators shall be final; if they do not agree the decision of the referee shall be final. If the parties fail to agree, upon the place of arbitration, it shall be The Hague, Holland.
Interpretation of Texts:	Contract written in Arabic and English language, each of which has equal validity.

INDEX